Sci

for

Everyday Living

Presented to:

_____

Given By:

_____

Date:

_____

SCRIPTURES

FOR

Everyday Living

Easily find any verse you need

ISBN: 979-8-9856215-0-1 (Paperback)
ISBN: 979-8-9856215-1-8 (E-Book)

Library of Congress Control Number: 2022901288

Front Cover Design by: Olivia Pro Design

Published by Visual Ministries, Fleming Island, FL. United States
Second edition 2023

Website: www.keithgwaltney.com

Stay connected with the author

Feedback-Products-Future books

Available now, Prayers for Everyday Living!

Visit website:
https://www.kgmagic.com/

Author's YouTube channel:
http://bit.ly/kgmagic

CONTENT

Introduction

Jesus answered, "It is written: 'Man shall not live on bread alone, but on every word that comes from the mouth of God."   Matthew 4:4 NIV

Life is going to be difficult at times no matter who you are. Being a Christian and having a relationship with God is not going to keep bad things or trouble from happening to you or around you. Knowing God's promise to us and staying in His Word can bring peace, joy, and an understanding that might otherwise not be known.

My goal is to give you a reference to God's Word on different circumstances that you may experience on any given day of your life. If you are worried, lonely, need strength, in grief or in need of truth, it is my prayer that you will be able to turn to God's Word and know that He is there with you and for you!

Keith Gwaltney

Anger

Cease from anger, and forsake wrath: fret not thyself in any wise to do evil. Psalm 37:8 KJV

Refrain from anger and turn from wrath; do not fret- it leads only to evil. Psalm 37:8 NIV

He that is slow to wrath is of great understanding: but he that is hasty of spirit exalteth folly.

Proverbs 14:29 KJV

Whoever is patient has great understanding, but one who is quick-tempered displays folly.

Proverbs 14:29 NIV

If thine enemy be hungry, give him bread to eat; and if he be thirsty, give him water to drink: For thou shalt heap coals of fire upon his head, and the Lord shall reward thee. Proverbs 25:21-22 KJV

If your enemy is hungry, give him food to eat; if he is thirsty give him water to drink. In doing this, you will heap burning coals on his head, and the Lord will reward you. Proverbs 25:21-22 NIV

Wherefore, my beloved brethren, let every man be swift to hear, slow to speak, slow to wrath: For the wrath of man worketh not the righteousness of God.

James 1:19-20 KJV

My dear brothers and sister, take not of this: Everyone should be quick to listen, slow to speak and slow to become angry, because human anger does not produce the righteousness that God desires.

James 1:19-20 NIV

A fool uttereth all his mind: but a wise man keepeth it in till afterwards.   Proverbs 29:11 KJV

Fools give full vent to their rage, but the wise bring calm in the end.   Proverbs 29:11 NIV

Dearly beloved, avenge not yourselves, but rather give place unto wrath: for it is written, Vengeance is mine; I will repay, saith the Lord.

Romans 12:19 KJV

Do not take revenge my dear friends, but leave room for God's wrath, for it is written: "It is mine to avenge; I will repay," says the Lord.

Romans 12:19 NIV

Anxiety

Be careful for nothing; but in every thing by prayer and supplication with thanksgiving let your requests be made known unto God. And the peace of God, which passeth all understanding, shall keep your hearts and minds through Christ Jesus.   Philippians 4:6-7 KJV

Do not be anxious about anything, but in every situation, by prayer and petition, with thanksgiving, present your requests to God. And the peace of God, which transcends all understanding, will guard your hearts and your minds in Christ Jesus.   Philippians 4:6-7 NIV

Have not I commanded thee? Be strong and of a good courage; be not afraid, neither be thou dismayed: for the Lord thy God is with thee whithersoever thou goest.
Joshua 1:9 KJV

Have I not commanded you? Be strong and courageous. Do not be afraid; do not be discouraged, for the Lord your God will be with you wherever you go.
Joshua 1:9 NIV

Heaviness in the heart of man maketh it stoop: but a good word maketh it glad.   Proverbs 12:25 KJV

Anxiety weighs down the heart, but a kind word cheers it up.   Proverbs 12:25 NIV

Therefore I say unto you, Take no thought for your life, what ye shall eat, or what ye shall drink; nor yet for your body, what ye shall put on. Is not the life more than meat, and the body than raiment? Behold the fowls of the air: for they sow not, neither do they reap, nor gather into barns; yet your heavenly Father feedeth them. Are ye not much better than they? Therefore take no thought, saying, What shall we eat? or, What shall we drink? or, Wherewithal shall we be clothed? (For after all these things do the Gentiles seek:) for your heavenly Father knoweth that ye have need of all these things. But seek ye first the kingdom of God, and his righteousness; and all these things shall be added unto you. Take therefore no thought for the morrow: for the morrow shall take thought for the things of itself. Sufficient unto the day is the evil thereof.　　　Matthew 6:25-26, 31-34 KJV

"Therefore I tell you, do not worry about your life, what you will eat or drink; or about your body, what you will wear. Is not life more than food, and the body more than clothes? Look at the birds of the air; they do not sow or reap or store away in barns, and yet your heavenly Father feeds them. Are you not much more valuable than they?" So do not worry, saying, 'What shall we eat?' or 'What shall we drink?' or 'What shall we wear?' For the pagans run after all these things, and your heavenly Father knows that you need them. But seek first his kingdom and his righteousness, and all these things will be given to you as well. Therefore do not worry about tomorrow, for tomorrow will worry about itself. Each day has enough trouble of its own.
Matthew 6:25-26, 31-34 NIV

Authority

You are of God, little children, and have overcome them, because He who is in you is greater than he who is in the world.

1 John 4:4 KJV

You, dear children, are from God and have overcome them, because the one who is in you is greater than the one who is in the world.

1 John 4:4 NIV

Let every soul be subject unto the higher powers. For there is no power but of God: the powers that be are ordained of God.

Romans 13:1 KJV

Let everyone be subject to the governing authorities, for there is no authority except that which God has established. The authorities that exist have been established by God.

Romans 13:1 NIV

And Jesus came and spoke to them, saying, "All authority has been given to Me in heaven and on earth."

Matthew 28:18 KJV

Then Jesus came to them and said, "All authority in heaven and on earth has been given to me."

Matthew 28:18 NIV

Knowing this first, that no prophecy of the scripture is of any private interpretation, for the prophecy came not in old time by the will of man: but holy men of God spake as they were moved by the Holy Ghost.

2 Peter 1:20-21 KJV

Above all, you must understand that no prophecy of Scripture came about by the prophet's own interpretation of things. For prophecy never had its origin in the human will, but prophets, through human, spoke from God as they were carried along by the Holy Spirit.

2 Peter 1:20-21 NIV

Behold, I give you the authority to trample on serpents and scorpions, and all over the power of the enemy, and nothing shall by any means hurt you.

Luke 10:19 KJV

I have given you authority to trample on snakes and scorpions and to overcome all the power of the enemy; nothing will harm you.

Luke 10:19 NIV

Every word of God is pure; He is a shield to those who put their trust in Him.   Proverbs 30:5 KJV

Every word of God is flawless; He is a shield to those who take refuge in Him.   Proverbs 30:5 NIV

Belief

For God so loved the world, that he gave his only begotten Son, that whosoever believeth in him should not perish, but have everlasting life.   John 3:16 KJV

For God so loved the world that he gave his one and only Son, that whoever believes in him shall not perish but have eternal life.   John 3:16 NIV

Let us hold fast the profession of our faith without wavering; (for he is faithful that promised;).
Hebrews 10:23 KJV

Let us hold unswervingly to the hope we profess, for he who promised is faithful.
Hebrews 10:23 NIV

And this is the confidence that we have in him, that, if we ask any thing according to his will, he heareth us: And if we know that he hear us, whatsoever we ask, we know that we have the petitions that we desired of him.
1 John 5:14-15 KJV

This is the confidence we have in approaching God: that if we ask anything according to his will, he hears us. [15] And if we know that he hears us—whatever we ask—we know that we have what we asked of him.
1 John 5:14-15 NIV

To him give all the prophets witness, that through his name whosoever believeth in him shall receive remission of sins.
Acts 10:43 KJV

All the prophets testify about him that everyone who believes in him receives forgiveness of sins through his name.
Acts 10:43 NIV

That if thou shalt confess with thy mouth the Lord Jesus, and shalt believe in thine heart that God hath raised him from the dead, thou shalt be saved. For with the heart man believeth unto righteousness; and with the mouth confession is made unto salvation.
Romans 10:9-10 KJV

If you declare with your mouth, "Jesus is Lord," and believe in your heart that God raised him from the dead, you will be saved. For it is with your heart that you believe and are justified, and it is with your mouth that you profess your faith and are saved.
Romans 10:9-10 NIV

But without faith it is impossible to please him: for he that cometh to God must believe that he is, and that he is a rewarder of them that diligently seek him.
Hebrews 11:6 KJV

And without faith it is impossible to please God, because anyone who comes to him must believe that he exists and that he rewards those who earnestly seek him.
Hebrews 11:6 NIV

Blessings

Every good gift and every perfect gift is from above, and cometh down from the Father of lights, with whom is no variableness, neither shadow of turning.

James 1:17 KJV

Every good and perfect gift is from above, coming down from the Father of the heavenly lights, who does not change like shifting shadows.

James 1:17 NIV

The Lord bless thee, and keep thee: The Lord make his face shine upon thee, and be gracious unto thee: The Lord lift up his countenance upon thee, and give thee peace.

Numbers 6:24-26 KJV

"The Lord bless you and keep you; the Lord make his face shine on you and be gracious to you; the Lord turn his face toward you and give you peace."

Numbers 6:24-26 NIV

Blessed is the man that trusteth in the Lord, and whose hope the Lord is.

Jeremiah 17:7 KJV

"But blessed is the one who trusts in the Lord, whose confidence is in him.

Jeremiah 17:7 NIV

And God is able to make all grace abound toward you; that ye, always having all sufficiency in all things, may abound to every good work.

2 Corinthians 9:8 KJV

And God is able to bless you abundantly, so that in all things at all times, having all that you need, you will abound in every good work.

2 Corinthians 9:8 NIV

Blessings are upon the head of the just: but violence covereth the mouth of the wicked.

Proverbs 10:6 KJV

Blessings crown the head of the righteous, but violence overwhelms the mouth of the wicked.

Proverbs 10:6 NIV

Blessed be the God and Father of our Lord Jesus Christ, who hath blessed us with all spiritual blessings in heavenly places in Christ.

Ephesians 1:3 KJV

Praise be to the God and Father of our Lord Jesus Christ, who has blessed us in the heavenly realms with every spiritual blessing in Christ.

Ephesians 1:3 NIV

Children

Train up a child in the way he should go, And when he is old he will not depart from it.

Proverbs 22:6 KJV

Start children off on the way they should go, and even when they are old they will not turn from it.

Proverbs 22:6 NIV

At the same time came the disciples unto Jesus, saying, Who is the greatest in the kingdom of heaven? And Jesus called a little child unto him, and set him in the midst of them, And said, Verily I say unto you, Except ye be converted, and become as little children, ye shall not enter into the kingdom of heaven. Whosoever therefore shall humble himself as this little child, the same is greatest in the kingdom of heaven.

Matthew 18:1-4 KJV

At that time the disciples came to Jesus and asked, "Who, then, is the greatest in the kingdom of heaven?" He called a little child to him, and placed the child among them. And he said: "Truly I tell you, unless you change and become like little children, you will never enter the kingdom of heaven. Therefore, whoever takes the lowly position of this child is the greatest in the kingdom of heaven.

Matthew 18:1-4 NIV

Lo, children are an heritage of the Lord: and the fruit of the womb is his reward.

Psalm 127:3 KJV

Children are a heritage from the Lord, offspring a reward from him.

Psalm 127:3 NIV

Before I formed thee in the belly I knew thee; and before thou camest forth out of the womb I sanctified thee, and I ordained thee a prophet unto the nations.

Jeremlah 1:5 KJV

"Before I formed you in the womb I knew you, before you were born I set you apart; I appointed you as a prophet to the nations."

Jeremiah 1:5 NIV

I have no greater joy than to hear that my children walk in truth.

3 John 1:4 KJV

I have no greater joy than to hear that my children are walking in the truth.

3 John 1:4 NIV

Church

Behold, how good and how pleasant it is for brethren to dwell together in unity!

Psalm 133:1 KJV

How good and pleasant it is when God's people live together in unity!

Psalm 133:1 NIV

For as we have many members in one body, and all members have not the same office: So we, being many, are one body in Christ, and every one members one of another.

Romans 12:4-5 KJV

For just as each of us has one body with many members, and these members do not all have the same function, so in Christ we, though many, form one body, and each member belongs to all the others.

Romans 12:4-5 NIV

For where two or three are gathered together in my name, there am I in the midst of them.

Matthew 18:20 KJV

"For where two or three gather in my name, there am I with them."

Matthew 18:20 NIV

And are built upon the foundation of the apostles and prophets, Jesus Christ himself being the chief corner stone; In whom all the building fitly framed together groweth unto an holy temple in the Lord: In whom ye also are builded together for an habitation of God through the Spirit.   Ephesians 2:20-22 KJV

Built on the foundation of the apostles and prophets, with Christ Jesus himself as the chief cornerstone. In him the whole building is joined together and rises to become a holy temple in the Lord. And in him you too are being built together to become a dwelling in which God lives by his Spirit.   Ephesians 2:20-22 NIV

For by one Spirit are we all baptized into one body, whether we be Jews or Gentiles, whether we be bond or free; and have been all made to drink into one Spirit.
1 Corinthians 12:13 KJV

For we were all baptized by one Spirit so as to form one body—whether Jews or Gentiles, slave or free—and we were all given the one Spirit to drink.
1 Corinthians 12:13 NIV

And there are differences of administrations, but the same Lord.   1 Corinthians 12:5 KJV

There are different kinds of service, but the same Lord.
1 Corinthians 12:5 NIV

15

Compassion

The Lord is not slack concerning his promise, as some men count slackness; but is longsuffering to us-ward, not willing that any should perish, but that all should come to repentance.

2 Peter 3:9 KJV

The Lord is not slow in keeping his promise, as some understand slowness. Instead he is patient with you, not wanting anyone to perish, but everyone to come to repentance.

2 Peter 3:9 NIV

Rejoice with them that do rejoice, and weep with them that weep.

Romans 12:15 KJV

Rejoice with those who rejoice; mourn with those who mourn.

Romans 12:15 NIV

Great are thy tender mercies, O Lord: quicken me according to thy judgments.

Psalm 119:156 KJV

Your compassion, Lord, is great; preserve my life according to your laws.

Psalm 119:156 NIV

It is of the Lord's mercies that we are not consumed, because his compassions fail not. They are new every morning: great is thy faithfulness.

Lamentations 3:22-23 KJV

Because of the Lord's great love we are not consumed, for his compassions never fail. They are new every morning; great is your faithfulness.

Lamentations 3:22-23 NIV

But the mercy of the Lord is from everlasting to everlasting upon them that fear him, and his righteousness unto children's children.

Psalm 103:17 KJV

But from everlasting to everlasting the Lord's love is with those who fear him, and his righteousness with their children's children.

Psalm 103:17 NIV

And therefore will the Lord wait, that he may be gracious unto you, and therefore will he be exalted, that he may have mercy upon you: for the Lord is a God of judgment: blessed are all they that wait for him.

Isaiah 30:18 KJV

Yet the Lord longs to be gracious to you; therefore he will rise up to show you compassion. For the Lord is a God of justice. Blessed are all who wait for him!

Isaiah 30:18 NIV

17

Condemned

Verily, verily, I say unto you, He that heareth my word, and believeth on him that sent me, hath everlasting life, and shall not come into condemnation; but is passed from death unto life.

John 5:24 KJV

"Very truly I tell you, whoever hears my word and believes him who sent me has eternal life and will not be judged but has crossed over from death to life.

John 5:24 NIV

For God sent not his Son into the world to condemn the world; but that the world through him might be saved. He that believeth on him is not condemned: but he that believeth not is condemned already, because he hath not believed in the name of the only begotten Son of God.

John 3:17-18 KJV

For God did not send his Son into the world to condemn the world, but to save the world through him. Whoever believes in him is not condemned, but whoever does not believe stands condemned already because they have not believed in the name of God's one and only Son.

John 3:17-18 NIV

Therefore if any man be in Christ, he is a new creature: old things are passed away; behold, all things are become new.

2 Corinthians 5:17 KJV

Therefore, if anyone is in Christ, the new creation has come: The old has gone, the new is here!

2 Corinthians 5:17 NIV

If we confess our sins, he is faithful and just to forgive us our sins, and to cleanse us from all unrighteousness.

1 John 1:9 KJV

If we confess our sins, he is faithful and just and will forgive us our sins and purify us from all unrighteousness.

1 John 1:9 NIV

Blessed is he whose transgression is forgiven, whose sin is covered.

Psalm 32:1 KJV

Blessed is the one whose transgressions are forgiven, whose sins are covered.

Psalm 32:1 NIV

Confidence

I can do all things through Christ which strengtheneth me.
Philippians 4:13 KJV

I can do all this through him who gives me strength.
Philippians 4:13 NIV

And such trust have we through Christ to God-ward: Not that we are sufficient of ourselves to think any thing as of ourselves; but our sufficiency is of God.
2 Corinthians 3:4-5 KJV

Such confidence we have through Christ before God. Not that we are competent in ourselves to claim anything for ourselves, but our competence comes from God.
2 Corinthians 3:4-5 NIV

So that we may boldly say, The Lord is my helper, and I will not fear what man shall do unto me.
Hebrews 13:6 KJV

So we say with confidence, "The Lord is my helper; I will not be afraid. What can mere mortals do to me?
Hebrews 13:6 NIV

Being confident of this very thing, that he which hath begun a good work in you will perform it until the day of Jesus Christ.   Philippians 1:6 KJV

Being confident of this, that he who began a good work in you will carry it on to completion until the day of Christ Jesus.   Philippians 1:6 NIV

Cast not away therefore your confidence, which hath great recompence of reward. For ye have need of patience, that, after ye have done the will of God, ye might receive the promise.

Hebrews 10:35-36 KJV

So do not throw away your confidence; it will be richly rewarded. You need to persevere so that when you have done the will of God, you will receive what he has promised.

Hebrews 10:35-36 NIV

Yea, though I walk through the valley of the shadow of death, I will fear no evil: for thou art with me; thy rod and thy staff they comfort me.   Psalm 23:4 KJV

Even though I walk through the darkest valley, I will fear no evil, for you are with me; your rod and your staff, they comfort me.   Psalm 23:4 NIV

Contentment

But godliness with contentment is great gain. For we brought nothing into this world, and it is certain we can carry nothing out.

1 Timothy 6:6-7 KJV

But godliness with contentment is great gain. For we brought nothing into the world, and we can take nothing out of it.

1 Timothy 6:6-7 NIV

But seek ye first the kingdom of God, and his righteousness; and all these things shall be added unto you.

Matthew 6:33 KJV

But seek first his kingdom and his righteousness, and all these things will be given to you as well.

Matthew 6:33 NIV

This is the day which the Lord hath made; we will rejoice and be glad in it.

Psalm 118:24 KJV

The Lord has done it this very day; let us rejoice today and be glad.

Psalm 118:24 NIV

And he said unto them, Take heed, and beware of covetousness: for a man's life consisteth not in the abundance of the things which he possesseth.

Luke 12:15 KJV

Then he said to them, "Watch out! Be on your guard against all kinds of greed; life does not consist in an abundance of possessions."

Luke 12:15 NIV

But my God shall supply all your need according to his riches in glory by Christ Jesus.

Philippians 4:19 KJV

And my God will meet all your needs according to the riches of his glory in Christ Jesus.

Philippians 4:19 NIV

Let your conversation be without covetousness; and be content with such things as ye have: for he hath said, I will never leave thee, nor forsake thee.

Hebrews 13:5 KJV

Keep your lives free from the love of money and be content with what you have, because God has said, "Never will I leave you; never will I forsake you."

Hebrews 13:5 NIV

Courage/Fear

Be strong and of a good courage, fear not, nor be afraid of them: for the Lord thy God, he it is that doth go with thee; he will not fail thee, nor forsake thee.

Deuteronomy 31:6 KJV

Be strong and courageous. Do not be afraid or terrified because of them, for the Lord your God goes with you; he will never leave you nor forsake you.

Deuteronomy 31:6 NIV

Fear thou not; for I am with thee: be not dismayed; for I am thy God: I will strengthen thee; yea, I will help thee; yea, I will uphold thee with the right hand of my righteousness.

Isaiah 41:10 KJV

So do not fear, for I am with you; do not be dismayed, for I am your God. I will strengthen you and help you; I will uphold you with my righteous right hand.

Isaiah 41:10 NIV

And immediately Jesus stretched forth his hand, and caught him, and said unto him, O thou of little faith, wherefore didst thou doubt?

Matthew 14:31 KJV

Immediately Jesus reached out his hand and caught him. "You of little faith," he said, "why did you doubt?"

Matthew 14:31 NIV

The Lord is my light and my salvation; whom shall I fear? the Lord is the strength of my life; of whom shall I be afraid?

Psalm 27:1 KJV

The Lord is my light and my salvation— whom shall I fear? The Lord is the stronghold of my life—of whom shall I be afraid?

Psalm 27:1 NIV

And fear not them which kill the body, but are not able to kill the soul: but rather fear him which is able to destroy both soul and body in hell.

Matthew 10:28 KJV

Do not be afraid of those who kill the body but cannot kill the soul. Rather, be afraid of the One who can destroy both soul and body in hell.

Matthew 10:28 NIV

When a man's ways please the Lord, he maketh even his enemies to be at peace with him.

Proverbs 16:7 KJV

When the Lord takes pleasure in anyone's way, he causes their enemies to make peace with them.

Proverbs 16:7 NIV

Decisions/Discernment

Call unto me, and I will answer thee, and show thee great and mighty things, which thou knowest not.

Jeremiah 33:3 KJV

Call to me and I will answer you and tell you great and unsearchable things you do not know.

Jeremiah 33:3 NIV

Howbeit when he, the Spirit of truth, is come, he will guide you into all truth: for he shall not speak of himself; but whatsoever he shall hear, that shall he speak: and he will shew you things to come.

John 16:13 KJV

But when he, the Spirit of truth, comes, he will guide you into all the truth. He will not speak on his own; he will speak only what he hears, and he will tell you what is yet to come.

John 16:13 NIV

Commit thy way unto the Lord; trust also in him; and he shall bring it to pass.

Psalm 37:5 KJV

Commit your way to the Lord; trust in him and he will do this.

Psalm 37:5 NIV

And I will pray the Father, and he shall give you another Comforter, that he may abide with you for ever; Even the Spirit of truth; whom the world cannot receive, because it seeth him not, neither knoweth him: but ye know him; for he dwelleth with you, and shall be in you.

John 14:16-17 KJV

And I will ask the Father, and he will give you another advocate to help you and be with you forever—the Spirit of truth. The world cannot accept him, because it neither sees him nor knows him. But you know him, for he lives with you and will be in you.   John 14:16-17 NIV

If any of you lack wisdom, let him ask of God, that giveth to all men liberally, and upbraideth not; and it shall be given him.   James 1:5 KJV

If any of you lacks wisdom, you should ask God, who gives generously to all without finding fault, and it will be given to you.   James 1:5 NIV

In all thy ways acknowledge him, and he shall direct thy paths.   Proverbs 3:6 KJV

In all your ways submit to him, and he will make your paths straight.   Proverbs 3:6 NIV

Deliverer

And it shall come to pass, that whosoever shall call on the name of the Lord shall be saved.

Acts 2:21 KJV

And everyone who calls on the name of the Lord will be saved.

Acts 2:21 NIV

For the law of the Spirit of life in Christ Jesus hath made me free from the law of sin and death.

Romans 8:2 KJV

Because through Christ Jesus the law of the Spirit who gives life has set you free from the law of sin and death.

Romans 8:2 NIV

These shall make war with the Lamb, and the Lamb shall overcome them: for he is Lord of lords, and King of kings: and they that are with him are called, and chosen, and faithful.

Revelation 17:14 KJV

They will wage war against the Lamb, but the Lamb will triumph over them because he is Lord of lords and King of kings—and with him will be his called, chosen and faithful followers.

Revelation 17:14 NIV

For I know that this shall turn to my salvation through your prayer, and the supply of the Spirit of Jesus Christ.

Philippians 1:19 KJV

For I know that through your prayers and God's provision of the Spirit of Jesus Christ what has happened to me will turn out for my deliverance.

Philippians 1:19 NIV

Behold, I give you the authority to trample on serpents and scorpions, and over all the power of the enemy, and nothing shall by any means hurt you.

Luke 10:19 KJV

I have given you authority to trample on snakes and scorpions and to overcome all the power of the enemy; nothing will harm you.

Luke 10:19 NIV

For God sent not his Son into the world to condemn the world; but that the world through him might be saved.

John 3:17 KJV

For God did not send his Son into the world to condemn the world, but to save the world through him.

John 3:17 NIV

Depression

Come unto me, all ye that labour and are heavy laden, and I will give you rest. Take my yoke upon you, and learn of me; for I am meek and lowly in heart: and ye shall find rest unto your souls. For my yoke is easy, and my burden is light.   Matthew 11:28-30 KJV

"Come to me, all you who are weary and burdened, and I will give you rest. Take my yoke upon you and learn from me, for I am gentle and humble in heart, and you will find rest for your souls. For my yoke is easy and my burden is light."   Matthew 11:28-30 NIV

The Lord also will be a refuge for the oppressed, a refuge in times of trouble. And they that know thy name will put their trust in thee: for thou, Lord, hast not forsaken them that seek thee.   Psalm 9:9-10 KJV

The Lord is a refuge for the oppressed, a stronghold in times of trouble. Those who know your name trust in you, for you, Lord, have never forsaken those who seek you.   Psalm 9:9-10 NIV

The Lord is nigh unto them that are of a broken heart; and saveth such as be of a contrite spirit. Psalm 34:18 KJV

The Lord is close to the brokenhearted and saves those who are crushed in spirit.   Psalm 34:18 NIV

And the Lord, he it is that doth go before thee; he will be with thee, he will not fail thee, neither forsake thee: fear not, neither be dismayed.

Deuteronomy 31:8 KJV

The LORD himself goes before you and will be with you; he will never leave you nor forsake you. Do not be afraid; do not be discouraged.

Deuteronomy 31:8 NIV

Fear thou not; for I am with thee: be not dismayed; for I am thy God: I will strengthen thee; yea, I will help thee; yea, I will uphold thee with the right hand of my righteousness.

Isaiah 41:10 KJV

So do not fear, for I am with you; do not be dismayed, for I am your God. I will strengthen you and help you; I will uphold you with my righteous right hand.

Isaiah 41:10 NIV

Yea, though I walk through the valley of the shadow of death, I will fear no evil: for thou art with me; thy rod and thy staff they comfort me.

Psalm 23:4 KJV

Even though I walk through the darkest valley, I will fear no evil, for you are with me; your rod and your staff, they comfort me.

Psalm 23:4 NIV

31

Discipleship

And Jesus came and spake unto them, saying, All power is given unto me in heaven and in earth. Go ye therefore, and teach all nations, baptizing them in the name of the Father, and of the Son, and of the Holy Ghost: Teaching them to observe all things whatsoever I have commanded you: and, lo, I am with you always, even unto the end of the world. Amen.

Matthew 28:18-20 KJV

Then Jesus came to them and said, "All authority in heaven and on earth has been given to me. Therefore go and make disciples of all nations, baptizing them in the name of the Father and of the Son and of the Holy Spirit, and teaching them to obey everything I have commanded you. And surely I am with you always, to the very end of the age."

Matthew 28:18-20 NIV

Then said Jesus to those Jews which believed on him, If ye continue in my word, then are ye my disciples indeed; And ye shall know the truth, and the truth shall make you free.   John 8:31-32 KJV

To the Jews who had believed him, Jesus said, "If you hold to my teaching, you are really my disciples. Then you will know the truth, and the truth will set you free."

John 8:31-32 NIV

And whosoever doth not bear his cross, and come after me, cannot be my disciple.

Luke 14:27 KJV

And whoever does not carry their cross and follow me cannot be my disciple.

Luke 14:27 NIV

The disciple is not above his master: but every one that is perfect shall be as his master.

Luke 6:40 KJV

The student is not above the teacher, but everyone who is fully trained will be like their teacher.

Luke 6:40 NIV

Ye are the light of the world. A city that is set on an hill cannot be hid. Neither do men light a candle, and put it under a bushel, but on a candlestick; and it giveth light unto all that are in the house. Let your light so shine before men, that they may see your good works, and glorify your Father which is in heaven.

Matthew 5:14-16 KJV

You are the light of the world. A town built on a hill cannot be hidden. Neither do people light a lamp and put it under a bowl. Instead they put it on its stand, and it gives light to everyone in the house. In the same way, let your light shine before others, that they may see your good deeds and glorify your Father in heaven.

Matthew 5:14-16 NIV

Discouraged

And let us not be weary in well doing: for in due season we shall reap, if we faint not.

Galatians 6:9 KJV

Let us not become weary in doing good, for at the proper time we will reap a harvest if we do not give up.

Galatians 6:9 NIV

Now the God of hope fill you with all joy and peace in believing, that ye may abound in hope, through the power of the Holy Ghost.

Romans 15:13 KJV

May the God of hope fill you with all joy and peace as you trust in him, so that you may overflow with hope by the power of the Holy Spirit.

Romans 15:13 NIV

If in this life only we have hope in Christ, we are of all men most miserable.

1 Corinthians 15:19 KJV

If only for this life we have hope in Christ, we are of all people most to be pitied.

1 Corinthians 15:19 NIV

Though I walk in the midst of trouble, thou wilt revive me: thou shalt stretch forth thine hand against the wrath of mine enemies, and thy right hand shall save me.

Psalm 138:7 KJV

Though I walk in the midst of trouble, you preserve my life. You stretch out your hand against the anger of my foes; with your right hand you save me.

Psalm 138:7 NIV

We are troubled on every side, yet not distressed; we are perplexed, but not in despair; Persecuted, but not forsaken; cast down, but not destroyed.

2 Corinthians 4:8-9 KJV

We are hard pressed on every side, but not crushed; perplexed, but not in despair; persecuted, but not abandoned; struck down, but not destroyed.

2 Corinthians 4:8-9 NIV

Hear me, O Lord; for thy lovingkindness is good: turn unto me according to the multitude of thy tender mercies.

Psalm 69:16 KJV

Answer me, Lord, out of the goodness of your love; in your great mercy turn to me.

Psalm 69:16 NIV

Encouragement

For I know the thoughts that I think toward you, saith the Lord, thoughts of peace, and not of evil, to give you an expected end.

Jeremiah 29:11 KJV

For I know the plans I have for you," declares the Lord, "plans to prosper you and not to harm you, plans to give you hope and a future.

Jeremiah 29:11 NIV

Cast thy burden upon the Lord, and he shall sustain thee: he shall never suffer the righteous to be moved.

Psalm 55:22 KJV

Cast your cares on the Lord and he will sustain you; he will never let the righteous be shaken.

Psalm 55:22 NIV

Lord, thou hast heard the desire of the humble: thou wilt prepare their heart, thou wilt cause thine ear to hear.

Psalm 10:17 KJV

You, Lord, hear the desire of the afflicted; you encourage them, and you listen to their cry.

Psalm 10:17 NIV

Have not I commanded thee? Be strong and of a good courage; be not afraid, neither be thou dismayed: for the Lord thy God is with thee whithersoever thou goest.

Joshua 1:9 KJV

Have I not commanded you? Be strong and courageous. Do not be afraid; do not be discouraged, for the Lord your God will be with you wherever you go.

Joshua 1:9 NIV

These things I have spoken unto you, that in me ye might have peace. In the world ye shall have tribulation: but be of good cheer; I have overcome the world.

John 16:33 KJV

"I have told you these things, so that in me you may have peace. In this world you will have trouble. But take heart! I have overcome the world."

John 16:33 NIV

For which cause we faint not; but though our outward man perish, yet the inward man is renewed day by day.

2 Corinthians 4:16 KJV

Therefore we do not lose heart. Though outwardly we are wasting away, yet inwardly we are being renewed day by day.

2 Corinthians 4:16 NIV

Eternal Life

For God so loved the world, that he gave his only begotten Son, that whosoever believeth in him should not perish, but have everlasting life.

John 3:16 KJV

For God so loved the world that he gave his one and only Son, that whoever believes in him shall not perish but have eternal life.

John 3:16 NIV

For the wages of sin is death; but the gift of God is eternal life through Jesus Christ our Lord.

Romans 6:23 KJV

For the wages of sin is death, but the gift of God is eternal life in Christ Jesus our Lord.

Romans 6:23 NIV

Surely goodness and mercy shall follow me all the days of my life: and I will dwell in the house of the Lord for ever.

Psalm 23:6 KJV

Surely your goodness and love will follow me all the days of my life, and I will dwell in the house of the Lord forever.

Psalm 23:6 NIV

For by grace are ye saved through faith; and that not of yourselves: it is the gift of God: Not of works, lest any man should boast.

Ephesians 2:8-9 KJV

For it is by grace you have been saved, through faith— and this is not from yourselves, it is the gift of God— not by works, so that no one can boast.

Ephesians 2:8-9 NIV

The Lord is not slack concerning his promise, as some men count slackness; but is longsuffering to us-ward, not willing that any should perish, but that all should come to repentance.

2 Peter 3:9 KJV

The Lord is not slow in keeping his promise, as some understand slowness. Instead he is patient with you, not wanting anyone to perish, but everyone to come to repentance.

2 Peter 3:9 NIV

And the world passeth away, and the lust thereof: but he that doeth the will of God abideth for ever.

1 John 2:17 KJV

The world and its desires pass away, but whoever does the will of God lives forever.

1 John 2:17 NIV

Faith

If any of you lack wisdom, let him ask of God, that giveth to all men liberally, and upbraideth not; and it shall be given him. But let him ask in faith, nothing wavering. For he that wavereth is like a wave of the sea driven with the wind and tossed. For let not that man think that he shall receive any thing of the Lord. A double minded man is unstable in all his ways.

James 1:5-8 KJV

If any of you lacks wisdom, you should ask God, who gives generously to all without finding fault, and it will be given to you. But when you ask, you must believe and not doubt, because the one who doubts is like a wave of the sea, blown and tossed by the wind. That person should not expect to receive anything from the Lord. Such a person is double-minded and unstable in all they do.

James 1:5-8 NIV

And all things, whatsoever ye shall ask in prayer, believing, ye shall receive.

Matthew 21:22 KJV

If you believe, you will receive whatever you ask for in prayer.

Matthew 21:22 NIV

But without faith it is impossible to please him: for he that cometh to God must believe that he is, and that he is a rewarder of them that diligently seek him.

Hebrews 11:6 KJV

And without faith it is impossible to please God, because anyone who comes to him must believe that he exists and that he rewards those who earnestly seek him.

Hebrews 11:6 NIV

Whom having not seen, ye love; in whom, though now ye see him not, yet believing, ye rejoice with joy unspeakable and full of glory.

1 Peter 1:8 KJV

Though you have not seen him, you love him; and even though you do not see him now, you believe in him and are filled with an inexpressible and glorious joy.

1 Peter 1:8 NIV

Verily, verily, I say unto you, He that believeth on me, the works that I do shall he do also; and greater works than these shall he do; because I go unto my Father.

John 14:12 KJV

Very truly I tell you, whoever believes in me will do the works I have been doing, and they will do even greater things than these, because I am going to the Father.

John 14:12 NIV

Fellowship

This then is the message which we have heard of him, and declare unto you, that God is light, and in him is no darkness at all. If we say that we have fellowship with him, and walk in darkness, we lie, and do not the truth: But if we walk in the light, as he is in the light, we have fellowship one with another, and the blood of Jesus Christ his Son cleanseth us from all sin.

1 John 1:5-7 KJV

This is the message we have heard from him and declare to you: God is light; in him there is no darkness at all. If we claim to have fellowship with him and yet walk in the darkness, we lie and do not live out the truth. But if we walk in the light, as he is in the light, we have fellowship with one another, and the blood of Jesus, his Son, purifies us from all sin.

1 John 1:5-7 NIV

For where two or three are gathered together in my name, there am I in the midst of them.

Matthew 18:20 KJV

For where two or three gather in my name, there am I with them.

Matthew 18:20 NIV

Two are better than one; because they have a good reward for their labour. For if they fall, the one will lift up his fellow: but woe to him that is alone when he falleth; for he hath not another to help him up. Again, if two lie together, then they have heat: but how can one be warm alone? And if one prevail against him, two shall withstand him; and a threefold cord is not quickly broken. Ecclesiastes 4:9-12 KJV

Two are better than one, because they have a good return for their labor: If either of them falls down, one can help the other up. But pity anyone who falls and has no one to help them up. Also, if two lie down together, they will keep warm. But how can one keep warm alone? Though one may be overpowered, two can defend themselves. A cord of three strands is not quickly broken. Ecclesiastes 4:9-12 NIV

Iron sharpeneth iron; so a man sharpeneth the countenance of his friend. Proverbs 27:17 KJV

As iron sharpens iron, so one person sharpens another. Proverbs 27:17 NIV

Be not deceived: evil communications corrupt good manners. 1 Corinthians 15:33 KJV

Do not be misled: "Bad company corrupts good character." 1 Corinthians 15:33 NIV

Finances

Therefore take no thought, saying, What shall we eat? or, What shall we drink? or, Wherewithal shall we be clothed? (For after all these things do the Gentiles seek:) for your heavenly Father knoweth that ye have need of all these things. But seek ye first the kingdom of God, and his righteousness; and all these things shall be added unto you.   Matthew 6:31-33 KJV

So do not worry, saying, 'What shall we eat?' or 'What shall we drink?' or 'What shall we wear?' For the pagans run after all these things, and your heavenly Father knows that you need them. But seek first his kingdom and his righteousness, and all these things will be given to you as well.   Matthew 6:31-33 NIV

Owe no man any thing, but to love one another: for he that loveth another hath fulfilled the law.
                                                                    Romans 13:8 KJV

Let no debt remain outstanding, except the continuing debt to love one another, for whoever loves others has fulfilled the law.   Romans 13:8 NIV

For where your treasure is, there will your heart be also.
                                                                    Matthew 6:21 KJV

For where your treasure is, there your heart will be also.
                                                                    Matthew 6:21 NIV

And he said unto them, Take heed, and beware of covetousness: for a man's life consisteth not in the abundance of the things which he possesseth.

Luke 12:15 KJV

Then he said to them, "Watch out! Be on your guard against all kinds of greed; life does not consist in an abundance of possessions."

Luke 12:15 NIV

Honour the Lord with thy substance, and with the firstfruits of all thine increase: So shall thy barns be filled with plenty, and thy presses shall burst out with new wine.

Proverbs 3:9-10 KJV

Honor the Lord with your wealth, with the firstfruits of all your crops; then your barns will be filled to overflowing, and your vats will brim over with new wine.

Proverbs 3:9-10 NIV

Give, and it shall be given unto you; good measure, pressed down, and shaken together, and running over, shall men give into your bosom. For with the same measure that ye mete withal it shall be measured to you again.

Luke 6:38 KJV

Give, and it will be given to you. A good measure, pressed down, shaken together and running over, will be poured into your lap. For with the measure you use, it will be measured to you.

Luke 6:38 NIV

Forgiveness

If we confess our sins, he is faithful and just to forgive us our sins, and to cleanse us from all unrighteousness.
1 John 1:9 KJV

If we confess our sins, he is faithful and just and will forgive us our sins and purify us from all unrighteousness.
1 John 1:9 NIV

And be ye kind one to another, tenderhearted, forgiving one another, even as God for Christ's sake hath forgiven you.
Ephesians 4:32 KJV

Be kind and compassionate to one another, forgiving each other, just as in Christ God forgave you.
Ephesians 4:32 NIV

And when ye stand praying, forgive, if ye have ought against any: that your Father also which is in heaven may forgive you your trespasses.
Mark 11:25 KJV

And when you stand praying, if you hold anything against anyone, forgive them, so that your Father in heaven may forgive you your sins.
Mark 11:25 NIV

Be it known unto you therefore, men and brethren, that through this man is preached unto you the forgiveness of sins: And by him all that believe are justified from all things, from which ye could not be justified by the law of Moses.   Acts 13:38-39 KJV

Therefore, my friends, I want you to know that through Jesus the forgiveness of sins is proclaimed to you. Through him everyone who believes is set free from every sin, a justification you were not able to obtain under the law of Moses.   Acts 13:38-39 NIV

For if ye forgive men their trespasses, your heavenly Father will also forgive you: But if ye forgive not men their trespasses, neither will your Father forgive your trespasses.   Matthew 6:14-15 KJV

For if you forgive other people when they sin against you, your heavenly Father will also forgive you. But if you do not forgive others their sins, your Father will not forgive your sins.   Matthew 6:14-15 NIV

For the wages of sin is death; but the gift of God is eternal life through Jesus Christ our Lord.
                                                    Romans 6:23 KJV

For the wages of sin is death, but the gift of God is eternal life in Christ Jesus our Lord.
                                                    Romans 6:23 NIV

Freedom

Now the Lord is that Spirit: and where the Spirit of the Lord is, there is liberty.

2 Corinthians 3:17 KJV

Now the Lord is the Spirit, and where the Spirit of the Lord is, there is freedom.

2 Corinthians 3:17 NIV

For the law of the Spirit of life in Christ Jesus hath made me free from the law of sin and death.

Romans 8:2 KJV

Because through Christ Jesus the law of the Spirit who gives life has set you free from the law of sin and death.

Romans 8:2 NIV

Then said Jesus to those Jews which believed on him, If ye continue in my word, then are ye my disciples indeed; And ye shall know the truth, and the truth shall make you free.

John 8:31-32 KJV

To the Jews who had believed him, Jesus said, "If you hold to my teaching, you are really my disciples. Then you will know the truth, and the truth will set you free."

John 8:31-32 NIV

While they promise them liberty, they themselves are the servants of corruption: for of whom a man is overcome, of the same is he brought in bondage.

2 Peter 2:19 KJV

They promise them freedom, while they themselves are slaves of depravity—for people are slaves to whatever has mastered them.

2 Peter 2:19 NIV

Jesus saith unto him, I am the way, the truth, and the life: no man cometh unto the Father, but by me.

John 14:6 KJV

Jesus answered, "I am the way and the truth and the life. No one comes to the Father except through me."

John 14:6 NIV

For the flesh lusteth against the Spirit, and the Spirit against the flesh: and these are contrary the one to the other: so that ye cannot do the things that ye would.

Galatians 5:17 KJV

For the flesh desires what is contrary to the Spirit, and the Spirit what is contrary to the flesh. They are in conflict with each other, so that you are not to do whatever you want.

Galatians 5:17 NIV

Future

Thy word is a lamp unto my feet, and a light unto my path.
Psalm 119:105 KJV

Your word is a lamp for my feet, a light on my path.
Psalm 119:105 NIV

Whereas ye know not what shall be on the morrow. For what is your life? It is even a vapour, that appeareth for a little time, and then vanisheth away. For that ye ought to say, If the Lord will, we shall live, and do this, or that.
James 4:14-15 KJV

Why, you do not even know what will happen tomorrow. What is your life? You are a mist that appears for a little while and then vanishes. Instead, you ought to say, "If it is the Lord's will, we will live and do this or that."
James 4:14-15 NIV

For I know the thoughts that I think toward you, saith the Lord, thoughts of peace, and not of evil, to give you an expected end.
Jeremiah 29:11 KJV

For I know the plans I have for you, declares the Lord, plans to prosper you and not to harm you, plans to give you hope and a future.
Jeremiah 29:11 NIV

But as it is written, Eye hath not seen, nor ear heard, neither have entered into the heart of man, the things which God hath prepared for them that love him. But God hath revealed them unto us by his Spirit: for the Spirit searcheth all things, yea, the deep things of God.
1 Corinthians 2:9-10 KJV

However, as it is written: "What no eye has seen, what no ear has heard and what no human mind has conceived"—the things God has prepared for those who love him—these are the things God has revealed to us by his Spirit. 1 Corinthians 2:9-10 NIV

There are many devices in a man's heart; nevertheless the counsel of the Lord, that shall stand.
Proverbs 19-21 KJV

Many are the plans in a person's heart, but it is the Lord's purpose that prevails. Proverbs 19:21 NIV

And God shall wipe away all tears from their eyes; and there shall be no more death, neither sorrow, nor crying, neither shall there be any more pain: for the former things are passed away. Revelations 21:4 KJV

He will wipe every tear from their eyes. There will be no more death or mourning or crying or pain, for the old order of things has passed away. Revelations 21:4 NIV

Giving

Every man according as he purposeth in his heart, so let him give; not grudgingly, or of necessity: for God loveth a cheerful giver.

2 Corinthians 9:7 KJV

Each of you should give what you have decided in your heart to give, not reluctantly or under compulsion, for God loves a cheerful giver.

2 Corinthians 9:7 NIV

The liberal soul shall be made fat: and he that watereth shall be watered also himself.

Proverbs 11:25 KJV

A generous person will prosper; whoever refreshes others will be refreshed.

Proverbs 11:25 NIV

Honour the Lord with thy substance, and with the firstfruits of all thine increase.

Proverbs 3:9 KJV

Honor the Lord with your wealth, with the firstfruits of all your crops.

Proverbs 3:9 NIV

But when thou doest alms, let not thy left hand know what thy right hand doeth: That thine alms may be in secret: and thy Father which seeth in secret himself shall reward thee openly.

Matthew 6:3-4 KJV

But when you give to the needy, do not let your left hand know what your right hand is doing, so that your giving may be in secret. Then your Father, who sees what is done in secret, will reward you.

Matthew 6:3-4 NIV

----------------------   ---

He that hath pity upon the poor lendeth unto the Lord; and that which he hath given will he pay him again.

Proverbs 19:17 KJV

Whoever is kind to the poor lends to the Lord, and he will reward them for what they have done.

Proverbs 19:17 NIV

Every good gift and every perfect gift is from above, and cometh down from the Father of lights, with whom is no variableness, neither shadow of turning.

James 1:17 KJV

Every good and perfect gift is from above, coming down from the Father of the heavenly lights, who does not change like shifting shadows.

James 1:17 NIV

Goals

The thoughts of the diligent tend only to plenteousness; but of every one that is hasty only to want.

Proverbs 21:5 KJV

The plans of the diligent lead to profit as surely as haste leads to poverty.

Proverbs 21:5 NIV

Know ye not that they which run in a race run all, but one receiveth the prize? So run, that ye may obtain. And every man that striveth for the mastery is temperate in all things. Now they do it to obtain a corruptible crown; but we an incorruptible. I therefore so run, not as uncertainly; so fight I, not as one that beateth the air: But I keep under my body, and bring it into subjection: lest that by any means, when I have preached to others, I myself should be a castaway.

1 Corinthians 9:24-27 KJV

Do you not know that in a race all the runners run, but only one gets the prize? Run in such a way as to get the prize. Everyone who competes in the games goes into strict training. They do it to get a crown that will not last, but we do it to get a crown that will last forever. Therefore I do not run like someone running aimlessly; I do not fight like a boxer beating the air. No, I strike a blow to my body and make it my slave so that after I have preached to others, I myself will not be disqualified for the prize.

1 Corinthians 9:24-27 NIV

Even so ye, forasmuch as ye are zealous of spiritual gifts, seek that ye may excel to the edifying of the church. 1 Corinthians 14:12 KJV

So it is with you. Since you are eager for gifts of the Spirit, try to excel in those that build up the church.
1 Corinthians 14:12 NIV

I can do all things through Christ which strengtheneth me. Philippians 4:13 KJV

I can do all this through him who gives me strength.
Philippians 4:13 NIV

I press toward the mark for the prize of the high calling of God in Christ Jesus. Let us therefore, as many as be perfect, be thus minded: and if in any thing ye be otherwise minded, God shall reveal even this unto you.
Philippians 3:14-15 KJV

I press on toward the goal to win the prize for which God has called me heavenward in Christ Jesus. All of us, then, who are mature should take such a view of things. And if on some point you think differently, that too God will make clear to you.
Philippians 3:14-15 NIV

Grace

For by grace are ye saved through faith; and that not of yourselves: it is the gift of God: Not of works, lest any man should boast.   Ephesians 2:8-9 KJV

For it is by grace you have been saved, through faith— and this is not from yourselves, it is the gift of God— not by works, so that no one can boast.
                                        Ephesians 2:8-9 NIV

For the law was given by Moses, but grace and truth came by Jesus Christ.
                                                    John 1:17 KJV

For the law was given through Moses; grace and truth came through Jesus Christ.
                                                    John 1:17 NIV

The Lord bless thee, and keep thee: The Lord make his face shine upon thee, and be gracious unto thee: The Lord lift up his countenance upon thee, and give thee peace.   Numbers 6:24-26 KJV

"The Lord bless you and keep you; the Lord make his face shine on you and be gracious to you; the Lord turn his face toward you and give you peace."
                                        Numbers 6:24-26 NIV

But the God of all grace, who hath called us unto his eternal glory by Christ Jesus, after that ye have suffered a while, make you perfect, stablish, strengthen, settle you.   1 Peter 5:10 KJV

And the God of all grace, who called you to his eternal glory in Christ, after you have suffered a little while, will himself restore you and make you strong, firm and steadfast.   1 Peter 5:10 NIV

And now, brethren, I commend you to God, and to the word of his grace, which is able to build you up, and to give you an inheritance among all them which are sanctified.   Acts 20:32 KJV

Now I commit you to God and to the word of his grace, which can build you up and give you an inheritance among all those who are sanctified.   Acts 20:32 NIV

For ye know the grace of our Lord Jesus Christ, that, though he was rich, yet for your sakes he became poor, that ye through his poverty might be rich.
2 Corinthians 8:9 KJV

For you know the grace of our Lord Jesus Christ, that though he was rich, yet for your sake he became poor, so that you through his poverty might become rich.
2 Corinthians 8:9 NIV

Grief

And God shall wipe away all tears from their eyes; and there shall be no more death, neither sorrow, nor crying, neither shall there be any more pain: for the former things are passed away.

Revelation 21:4 KJV

He will wipe every tear from their eyes. There will be no more death or mourning or crying or pain, for the old order of things has passed away.

Revelation 21:4 NIV

Blessed are they that mourn: for they shall be comforted.

Matthew 5:4 KJV

Blessed are those who mourn, for they will be comforted.

Matthew 5:4 NIV

The Lord is nigh unto them that are of a broken heart; and saveth such as be of a contrite spirit.

Psalm 34:18 KJV

The Lord is close to the brokenhearted and saves those who are crushed in spirit.

Psalm 34:18 NIV

But I would not have you to be ignorant, brethren, concerning them which are asleep, that ye sorrow not, even as others which have no hope. For if we believe that Jesus died and rose again, even so them also which sleep in Jesus will God bring with him. For this we say unto you by the word of the Lord, that we which are alive and remain unto the coming of the Lord shall not prevent them which are asleep. For the Lord himself shall descend from heaven with a shout, with the voice of the archangel, and with the trump of God: and the dead in Christ shall rise first: Then we which are alive and remain shall be caught up together with them in the clouds, to meet the Lord in the air: and so shall we ever be with the Lord. Wherefore comfort one another with these words.   1 Thessalonians 4:13-18 KJV

Brothers and sisters, we do not want you to be uninformed about those who sleep in death, so that you do not grieve like the rest of mankind, who have no hope. For we believe that Jesus died and rose again, and so we believe that God will bring with Jesus those who have fallen asleep in him. According to the Lord's word, we tell you that we who are still alive, who are left until the coming of the Lord, will certainly not precede those who have fallen asleep. For the Lord himself will come down from heaven, with a loud command, with the voice of the archangel and with the trumpet call of God, and the dead in Christ will rise first. After that, we who are still alive and are left will be caught up together with them in the clouds to meet the Lord in the air. And so we will be with the Lord forever. Therefore encourage one another with these words. 1 Thessalonians 4:13-18 NIV

Guidance

The steps of a good man are ordered by the Lord: and he delighteth in his way. Though he fall, he shall not be utterly cast down: for the Lord upholdeth him with his hand.   Psalm 37:23-24 KJV

The Lord makes firm the steps of the one who delights in him; though he may stumble, he will not fall, for the Lord upholds him with his hand.   Psalm 37:23-24 NIV

Ask, and it shall be given you; seek, and ye shall find; knock, and it shall be opened unto you: For every one that asketh receiveth; and he that seeketh findeth; and to him that knocketh it shall be opened.   Matthew 7:7-8 KJV

Ask and it will be given to you; seek and you will find; knock and the door will be opened to you. For everyone who asks receives; the one who seeks finds; and to the one who knocks, the door will be opened.
                                       Matthew 7:7-8 NIV

Thy word is a lamp unto my feet, and a light unto my path.   Psalm 119:105 KJV

Your word is a lamp for my feet, a light on my path.
                                       Psalm 119:105 NIV

And I will bring the blind by a way that they knew not; I will lead them in paths that they have not known: I will make darkness light before them, and crooked things straight. These things will I do unto them, and not forsake them. Isaiah 42:16 KJV

I will lead the blind by ways they have not known, along unfamiliar paths I will guide them; I will turn the darkness into light before them and make the rough places smooth. These are the things I will do; I will not forsake them. Isaiah 42:16 NIV

------- --

Shew me thy ways, O Lord; teach me thy paths. Lead me in thy truth, and teach me: for thou art the God of my salvation; on thee do I wait all the day.
Psalm 25:4-5 KJV

Show me your ways, Lord, teach me your paths. Guide me in your truth and teach me, for you are God my Savior, and my hope is in you all day long.
Psalm 25:4-5 NIV

For as many as are led by the Spirit of God, they are the sons of God. Romans 8:14 KJV

For those who are led by the Spirit of God are the children of God. Romans 8:14 NIV

Healing/Sickness

Is any sick among you? let him call for the elders of the church; and let them pray over him, anointing him with oil in the name of the Lord: And the prayer of faith shall save the sick, and the Lord shall raise him up; and if he have committed sins, they shall be forgiven him.

James 5:14-15 KJV

Is anyone among you sick? Let them call the elders of the church to pray over them and anoint them with oil in the name of the Lord. 15 And the prayer offered in faith will make the sick person well; the Lord will raise them up. If they have sinned, they will be forgiven.

James 5:14-15 NIV

A merry heart doeth good like a medicine: but a broken spirit drieth the bones.   Proverbs 17:22 KJV

A cheerful heart is good medicine, but a crushed spirit dries up the bones.   Proverbs 17:22 NIV

He healeth the broken in heart, and bindeth up their wounds.   Psalm 147:3 KJV

He heals the brokenhearted and binds up their wounds.

Psalm 147:3 NIV

If my people, which are called by my name, shall humble themselves, and pray, and seek my face, and turn from their wicked ways; then will I hear from heaven, and will forgive their sin, and will heal their land.   2 Chronicles 7:14 KJV

If my people, who are called by my name, will humble themselves and pray and seek my face and turn from their wicked ways, then I will hear from heaven, and I will forgive their sin and will heal their land.
                                                   2 Chronicles 7:14 NIV

Come, and let us return unto the Lord: for he hath torn, and he will heal us; he hath smitten, and he will bind us up.   Hosea 6:1 KJV

Come, let us return to the Lord. He has torn us to pieces but he will heal us; he has injured us but he will bind up our wounds.   Hosea 6:1 NIV

Beloved, I wish above all things that thou mayest prosper and be in health, even as thy soul prospereth.
                                                   3 John 1:2 KJV

Dear friend, I pray that you may enjoy good health and that all may go well with you, even as your soul is getting along well.   3 John 1:2 NIV

Heaven

In my Father's house are many mansions: if it were not so, I would have told you. I go to prepare a place for you. And if I go and prepare a place for you, I will come again, and receive you unto myself; that where I am, there ye may be also.

My Father's house has many rooms; if that were not so, would I have told you that I am going there to prepare a place for you? And if I go and prepare a place for you, I will come back and take you to be with me that you also may be where I am.

John 14:2-3 NIV

Lay not up for yourselves treasures upon earth, where moth and rust doth corrupt, and where thieves break through and steal: But lay up for yourselves treasures in heaven, where neither moth nor rust doth corrupt, and where thieves do not break through nor steal: For where your treasure is, there will your heart be also.

Matthew 6:19-21 KJV

Do not store up for yourselves treasures on earth, where moths and vermin destroy, and where thieves break in and steal. But store up for yourselves treasures in heaven, where moths and vermin do not destroy, and where thieves do not break in and steal. For where your treasure is, there your heart will be also.

Matthew 6:19-21 NIV

And the twelve gates were twelve pearls: every several gate was of one pearl: and the street of the city was pure gold, as it were transparent glass. And I saw no temple therein: for the Lord God Almighty and the Lamb are the temple of it. And the city had no need of the sun, neither of the moon, to shine in it: for the glory of God did lighten it, and the Lamb is the light thereof. And the nations of them which are saved shall walk in the light of it: and the kings of the earth do bring their glory and honour into it. And the gates of it shall not be shut at all by day: for there shall be no night there.

Revelation 21:21-25 KJV

The twelve gates were twelve pearls, each gate made of a single pearl. The great street of the city was of gold, as pure as transparent glass. I did not see a temple in the city, because the Lord God Almighty and the Lamb are its temple. The city does not need the sun or the moon to shine on it, for the glory of God gives it light, and the Lamb is its lamp. The nations will walk by its light, and the kings of the earth will bring their splendor into it. On no day will its gates ever be shut, for there will be no night there.

Revelation 21:21-25 NIV

For our conversation is in heaven; from whence also we look for the Saviour, the Lord Jesus Christ.

Philippians 3:20 KJV

But our citizenship is in heaven. And we eagerly await a Savior from there, the Lord Jesus Christ.

Philippians 3:20 NIV

Holiness

And the very God of peace sanctify you wholly; and I pray God your whole spirit and soul and body be preserved blameless unto the coming of our Lord Jesus Christ. 1 Thessalonians 5:23 KJV

May God himself, the God of peace, sanctify you through and through. May your whole spirit, soul and body be kept blameless at the coming of our Lord Jesus Christ. 1 Thessalonians 5:23 NIV

But ye are a chosen generation, a royal priesthood, an holy nation, a peculiar people; that ye should shew forth the praises of him who hath called you out of darkness into his marvellous light. 1 Peter 2:9 KJV

But you are a chosen people, a royal priesthood, a holy nation, God's special possession, that you may declare the praises of him who called you out of darkness into his wonderful light. 1 Peter 2:9 NIV

For God hath not called us unto uncleanness, but unto holiness. 1 Thessalonians 4:7 KJV

For God did not call us to be impure, but to live a holy life. 1 Thessalonians 4:7 NIV

As obedient children, not fashioning yourselves according to the former lusts in your ignorance: But as he which hath called you is holy, so be ye holy in all manner of conversation; Because it is written, Be ye holy; for I am holy.   1 Peter 1:14-16 KJV

As obedient children, do not conform to the evil desires you had when you lived in ignorance. But just as he who called you is holy, so be holy in all you do; 16 for it is written: "Be holy, because I am holy."
                                                    1 Peter 1:14-16 NIV

The righteousness of the perfect shall direct his way: but the wicked shall fall by his own wickedness.
                                                    Proverbs 11:5 KJV

The righteousness of the blameless makes their paths straight, but the wicked are brought down by their own wickedness.   Proverbs 11:5 NIV

Sanctify them through thy truth: thy word is truth.
                                                    John 17:17 KJV

Sanctify them by the truth; your word is truth.
                                                    John 17:17 NIV

Hope

This I recall to my mind, therefore have I hope. It is of the Lord's mercies that we are not consumed, because his compassions fail not.

Lamentations 3:21-22 KJV

Yet this I call to mind and therefore I have hope: because of the Lord's great love we are not consumed, for his compassions never fail.

Lamentations 3:21-22 NIV

Now the God of hope fill you with all joy and peace in believing, that ye may abound in hope, through the power of the Holy Ghost.

Romans 15:13 KJV

May the God of hope fill you with all joy and peace as you trust in him, so that you may overflow with hope by the power of the Holy Spirit.

Romans 15:13 NIV

Rejoicing in hope; patient in tribulation; continuing instant in prayer.

Romans 12:12 KJV

Be joyful in hope, patient in affliction, faithful in prayer.

Romans 12:12 NIV

68

And now, Lord, what wait I for? my hope is in thee.
Psalm 39:7 KJV

But now, Lord, what do I look for? My hope is in you.
Psalm 39:7 NIV

But they that wait upon the Lord shall renew their strength; they shall mount up with wings as eagles; they shall run, and not be weary; and they shall walk, and not faint. Isaiah 40:31 KJV

But those who hope in the Lord will renew their strength.
They will soar on wings like eagles; they will run and not grow weary, they will walk and not be faint.
Isaiah 40:31 NIV

That being justified by his grace, we should be made heirs according to the hope of eternal life.
Titus 3:7 KJV

So that, having been justified by his grace, we might become heirs having the hope of eternal life.
Titus 3:7 NIV

Identity

So God created man in his own image, in the image of God created he him; male and female created he them.

Genesis 1:27 KJV

So God created mankind in his own image, in the image of God he created them; male and female he created them.

Genesis 1:27 NIV

Before I formed thee in the belly I knew thee; and before thou camest forth out of the womb I sanctified thee, and I ordained thee a prophet unto the nations.

Jeremiah 1:5 KJV

"Before I formed you in the womb I knew you, before you were born I set you apart; I appointed you as a prophet to the nations."

Jeremiah 1:5 NIV

Therefore if any man be in Christ, he is a new creature: old things are passed away; behold, all things are become new.

2 Corinthians 5:17 KJV

Therefore, if anyone is in Christ, the new creation has come: The old has gone, the new is here!

2 Corinthians 5:17 NIV

Know ye that the Lord he is God: it is he that hath made us, and not we ourselves; we are his people, and the sheep of his pasture.   Psalm 100:3 KJV

Know that the Lord is God. It is he who made us, and we are his; we are his people, the sheep of his pasture.
                                                    Psalm 100:3 NIV

But ye are a chosen generation, a royal priesthood, an holy nation, a peculiar people; that ye should shew forth the praises of him who hath called you out of darkness into his marvellous light.
                                                    1 Peter 2:9 KJV

But you are a chosen people, a royal priesthood, a holy nation, God's special possession, that you may declare the praises of him who called you out of darkness into his wonderful light.
                                                    1 Peter 2:9 NIV

For our conversation is in heaven; from whence also we look for the Saviour, the Lord Jesus Christ.
                                                    Philippians 3:20 KJV

But our citizenship is in heaven. And we eagerly await a Savior from there, the Lord Jesus Christ.
                                                    Philippians 3:20 NIV

Joy

Thou hast loved righteousness, and hated iniquity; therefore God, even thy God, hath anointed thee with the oil of gladness above thy fellows.   Hebrews 1:9 KJV

You have loved righteousness and hated wickedness; therefore God, your God, has set you above your companions by anointing you with the oil of joy.

Hebrews 1:9 NIV

For thou, Lord, hast made me glad through thy work: I will triumph in the works of thy hands.

Psalm 92:4 KJV

For you make me glad by your deeds, Lord; I sing for joy at what your hands have done.

Psalm 92:4 NIV

But the fruit of the Spirit is love, joy, peace, longsuffering, gentleness, goodness, faith, Meekness, temperance: against such there is no law.

Galatians 5:22-23 KJV

But the fruit of the Spirit is love, joy, peace, forbearance, kindness, goodness, faithfulness, gentleness and self-control. Against such things there is no law.

Galatians 5:22-23 NIV

My brethren, count it all joy when ye fall into divers temptations; Knowing this, that the trying of your faith worketh patience. James 1:2-3 KJV

Consider it pure joy, my brothers and sisters, whenever you face trials of many kinds, because you know that the testing of your faith produces perseverance. James 1:2-3 NIV

For his anger endureth but a moment; in his favour is life: weeping may endure for a night, but joy cometh in the morning. Psalm 30:5 KJV

For his anger lasts only a moment, but his favor lasts a lifetime; weeping may stay for the night, but rejoicing comes in the morning. Psalm 30:5 NIV

For the kingdom of God is not meat and drink; but righteousness, and peace, and joy in the Holy Ghost. Romans 14:17 KJV

For the kingdom of God is not a matter of eating and drinking, but of righteousness, peace and joy in the Holy Spirit. Romans 14:17 NIV

Life

Then spake Jesus again unto them, saying, I am the light of the world: he that followeth me shall not walk in darkness, but shall have the light of life.   John 8:12 KJV

When Jesus spoke again to the people, he said, "I am the light of the world. Whoever follows me will never walk in darkness, but will have the light of life."
John 8:12 NIV

I am crucified with Christ: nevertheless I live; yet not I, but Christ liveth in me: and the life which I now live in the flesh I live by the faith of the Son of God, who loved me, and gave himself for me.   Galatians 2:20 KJV

I have been crucified with Christ and I no longer live, but Christ lives in me. The life I now live in the body, I live by faith in the Son of God, who loved me and gave himself for me.   Galatians 2:20 NIV

For the wages of sin is death; but the gift of God is eternal life through Jesus Christ our Lord.
Romans 6:23 KJV

For the wages of sin is death, but the gift of God is eternal life in Christ Jesus our Lord.
Romans 6:23 NIV

Jesus said unto her, I am the resurrection, and the life: he that believeth in me, though he were dead, yet shall he live: And whosoever liveth and believeth in me shall never die. Believest thou this?   John 11:25-26 KJV

Jesus said to her, "I am the resurrection and the life. The one who believes in me will live, even though they die; and whoever lives by believing in me will never die. Do you believe this?"   John 11:25-26 NIV

Jesus saith unto him, I am the way, the truth, and the life: no man cometh unto the Father, but by me.
John 14:6 KJV

Jesus answered, "I am the way and the truth and the life. No one comes to the Father except through me."
John 14:6 NIV

Fight the good fight of faith, lay hold on eternal life, whereunto thou art also called, and hast professed a good profession before many witnesses.
1 Timothy 6:12 KJV

Fight the good fight of the faith. Take hold of the eternal life to which you were called when you made your good confession in the presence of many witnesses.
1 Timothy 6:12 NIV

Lonely

The Lord is my shepherd; I shall not want. He maketh me to lie down in green pastures: he leadeth me beside the still waters. He restoreth my soul: he leadeth me in the paths of righteousness for his name's sake. Yea, though I walk through the valley of the shadow of death, I will fear no evil: for thou art with me; thy rod and thy staff they comfort me. Thou preparest a table before me in the presence of mine enemies: thou anointest my head with oil; my cup runneth over. Surely goodness and mercy shall follow me all the days of my life: and I will dwell in the house of the Lord for ever.   Psalm 23:1-6 KJV

The Lord is my shepherd, I lack nothing. He makes me lie down in green pastures, he leads me beside quiet waters, he refreshes my soul. He guides me along the right paths for his name's sake. Even though I walk through the darkest valley, I will fear no evil, for you are with me; your rod and your staff, they comfort me. You prepare a table before me in the presence of my enemies. You anoint my head with oil; my cup overflows. Surely your goodness and love will follow me all the days of my life, and I will dwell in the house of the Lord forever.   Psalm 23:1-6 NIV

I will not leave you comfortless: I will come to you.
John 14:18 KJV

I will not leave you as orphans; I will come to you.
John 14:18 NIV

Humble yourselves therefore under the mighty hand of God, that he may exalt you in due time: Casting all your care upon him; for he careth for you.

1 Peter 5:6-7 KJV

Humble yourselves, therefore, under God's mighty hand, that he may lift you up in due time. Cast all your anxiety on him because he cares for you.

1 Peter 5:6-7 NIV

There shall not any man be able to stand before thee all the days of thy life: as I was with Moses, so I will be with thee: I will not fail thee, nor forsake thee.

Joshua 1:5 KJV

No one will be able to stand against you all the days of your life. As I was with Moses, so I will be with you; I will never leave you nor forsake you.

Joshua 1:5 NIV

The Lord is nigh unto all them that call upon him, to all that call upon him in truth.

Psalm 145:18 KJV

The Lord is near to all who call on him, to all who call on him in truth.

Psalm 145:18 NIV

Love

Beloved, let us love one another: for love is of God; and every one that loveth is born of God, and knoweth God. He that loveth not knoweth not God; for God is love.

1 John 4:7-8 KJV

Dear friends, let us love one another, for love comes from God. Everyone who loves has been born of God and knows God. Whoever does not love does not know God, because God is love.

1 John 4:7-8 NIV

We love him, because he first loved us.

1 John 4:19 KJV

We love because he first loved us.

1 John 4:19 NIV

And above all things have fervent charity among yourselves: for charity shall cover the multitude of sins.

1 Peter 4:8 KJV

Above all, love each other deeply, because love covers over a multitude of sins.

1 Peter 4:8 NIV

And thou shalt love the Lord thy God with all thy heart, and with all thy soul, and with all thy mind, and with all thy strength: this is the first commandment. And the second is like, namely this, Thou shalt love thy neighbour as thyself. There is none other commandment greater than these.   Mark 12:30-31 KJV

Love the Lord your God with all your heart and with all your soul and with all your mind and with all your strength.' The second is this: 'Love your neighbor as yourself.' There is no commandment greater than these.
                                                      Mark 12:30-31 NIV

Charity suffereth long, and is kind; charity envieth not; charity vaunteth not itself, is not puffed up, Doth not behave itself unseemly, seeketh not her own, is not easily provoked, thinketh no evil; ejoiceth not in iniquity, but rejoiceth in the truth; Beareth all things, believeth all things, hopeth all things, endureth all things.
                                             1 Corinthians 13:4-7 KJV

Love is patient, love is kind. It does not envy, it does not boast, it is not proud. It does not dishonor others, it is not self-seeking, it is not easily angered, it keeps no record of wrongs. Love does not delight in evil but rejoices with the truth. It always protects, always trusts, always hopes, always perseveres.
                                             1 Corinthians 13:4-7 NIV

Marriage

Marriage is honourable in all, and the bed undefiled: but whoremongers and adulterers God will judge.

Hebrews 13:4 KJV

Marriage should be honored by all, and the marriage bed kept pure, for God will judge the adulterer and all the sexually immoral.

Hebrews 13:4 NIV

Be ye not unequally yoked together with unbelievers: for what fellowship hath righteousness with unrighteousness? and what communion hath light with darkness?

2 Corinthians 6:14 KJV

Do not be yoked together with unbelievers. For what do righteousness and wickedness have in common? Or what fellowship can light have with darkness?

2 Corinthians 6:14 NIV

Whoso findeth a wife findeth a good thing, and obtaineth favour of the Lord.

Proverbs 18:22 KJV

He who finds a wife finds what is good and receives favor from the Lord.

Proverbs 18:22 NIV

Wives, submit yourselves unto your own husbands, as unto the Lord. For the husband is the head of the wife, even as Christ is the head of the church: and he is the saviour of the body. Therefore as the church is subject unto Christ, so let the wives be to their own husbands in every thing. Husbands, love your wives, even as Christ also loved the church, and gave himself for it; That he might sanctify and cleanse it with the washing of water by the word. Ephesians 5:22-26 KJV

Wives, submit yourselves to your own husbands as you do to the Lord. For the husband is the head of the wife as Christ is the head of the church, his body, of which he is the Savior. Now as the church submits to Christ, so also wives should submit to their husbands in everything. Husbands, love your wives, just as Christ loved the church and gave himself up for her to make her holy, cleansing her by the washing with water through the word. Ephesians 5:22-26 NIV

And they twain shall be one flesh: so then they are no more twain, but one flesh. What therefore God hath joined together, let not man put asunder.
Mark 10:8-9 KJV

And the two will become one flesh. So they are no longer two, but one flesh. Therefore what God has joined together, let no one separate.
Mark 10:8-9 NIV

Meditation

This book of the law shall not depart out of thy mouth; but thou shalt meditate therein day and night, that thou mayest observe to do according to all that is written therein: for then thou shalt make thy way prosperous, and then thou shalt have good success.   Joshua 1:8 KJV

Keep this Book of the Law always on your lips; meditate on it day and night, so that you may be careful to do everything written in it. Then you will be prosperous and successful.   Joshua 1:8 NIV

We have thought of thy lovingkindness, O God, in the midst of thy temple.   Psalm 48:9 KJV

Within your temple, O God, we meditate on your unfailing love.   Psalm 48:9 NIV

My meditation of him shall be sweet: I will be glad in the Lord.   Psalm 104:34 KJV

May my meditation be pleasing to him, as I rejoice in the Lord.   Psalm 104:34 NIV

Till I come, give attendance to reading, to exhortation, to doctrine. Neglect not the gift that is in thee, which was given thee by prophecy, with the laying on of the hands of the presbytery. Meditate upon these things; give thyself wholly to them; that thy profiting may appear to all.   1 Timothy 4:13-15 KJV

Until I come, devote yourself to the public reading of Scripture, to preaching and to teaching. Do not neglect your gift, which was given you through prophecy when the body of elders laid their hands on you. Be diligent in these matters; give yourself wholly to them, so that everyone may see your progress.   1 Timothy 4:13-15 NIV

But his delight is in the law of the Lord; and in his law doth he meditate day and night.   Psalm 1:2 KJV

But whose delight is in the law of the Lord, and who meditates on his law day and night.   Psalm 1:2 NIV

My son, attend to my words; incline thine ear unto my sayings. Let them not depart from thine eyes; keep them in the midst of thine heart. For they are life unto those that find them, and health to all their flesh.
                                          Proverbs 4:20-22 KJV

My son, pay attention to what I say; turn your ear to my words. Do not let them out of your sight, keep them within your heart; for they are life to those who find them.   Proverbs 4:20-22 NIV

Mercy

Not by works of righteousness which we have done, but according to his mercy he saved us, by the washing of regeneration, and renewing of the Holy Ghost; Which he shed on us abundantly through Jesus Christ our Saviour.

Titus 3:5-6 KJV

He saved us, not because of righteous things we had done, but because of his mercy. He saved us through the washing of rebirth and renewal by the Holy Spirit, whom he poured out on us generously through Jesus Christ our Savior.

Titus 3:5-6 NIV

Be ye therefore merciful, as your Father also is merciful.

Luke 6:36 KJV

Be merciful, just as your Father is merciful.

Luke 6:36 NIV

And his mercy is on them that fear him from generation to generation.

Luke 1:50 KJV

His mercy extends to those who fear him, from generation to generation.

Luke 1:50 NIV

(For the Lord thy God is a merciful God;) he will not forsake thee, neither destroy thee, nor forget the covenant of thy fathers which he sware unto them.

Deuteronomy 4:31 KJV

For the Lord your God is a merciful God; he will not abandon or destroy you or forget the covenant with your ancestors, which he confirmed to them by oath.

Deuteronomy 4:31 NIV

It is of the Lord's mercies that we are not consumed, because his compassions fail not. They are new every morning: great is thy faithfulness.

Lamentations 3:22-23 KJV

Because of the Lord's great love we are not consumed, for his compassions never fail. They are new every morning; great is your faithfulness.

Lamentations 3:22-23 NIV

For he shall have judgment without mercy, that hath shewed no mercy; and mercy rejoiceth against judgment.

James 2:13 KJV

Because judgment without mercy will be shown to anyone who has not been merciful. Mercy triumphs over judgment.

James 2:13 NIV

Obedience

If ye love Me, keep My commandments.

John 14:15 KJV

If you love me, keep my commands.

John 14:15 NIV

For not the hearers of the law are just before God, but the doers of the law shall be justified.

Romans 2:13 KJV

For it is not those who hear the law who are righteous in God's sight, but it is those who obey the law who will be declared righteous.

Romans 2:13 NIV

For as by one man's disobedience many were made sinners, so by the obedience of one shall many be made righteous.   Romans 5:19 KJV

For just as through the disobedience of the one man the many were made sinners, so also through the obedience of the one man the many will be made righteous.

Romans 5:19 NIV

But whoso keepeth his word, in him verily is the love of God perfected: hereby know we that we are in him. He that saith he abideth in him ought himself also so to walk, even as he walked. 1 John 2:5-6 KJV

But if anyone obeys his word, love for God is truly made complete in them. This is how we know we are in him: Whoever claims to live in him must live as Jesus did. 1 John 2:5-6 NIV

As obedient children, not fashioning yourselves according to the former lusts in your ignorance.
1 Peter 1:14 KJV

As obedient children, do not conform to the evil desires you had when you lived in ignorance. 1 Peter 1:14 NIV

Whosoever therefore shall break one of these least commandments, and shall teach men so, he shall be called the least in the kingdom of heaven: but whosoever shall do and teach them, the same shall be called great in the kingdom of heaven. Matthew 5:19 KJV

Therefore anyone who sets aside one of the least of these commands and teaches others accordingly will be called least in the kingdom of heaven, but whoever practices and teaches these commands will be called great in the kingdom of heaven. Matthew 5:19 NIV

Patience

Be patient therefore, brethren, unto the coming of the Lord. Behold, the husbandman waiteth for the precious fruit of the earth, and hath long patience for it, until he receive the early and latter rain. Be ye also patient; stablish your hearts: for the coming of the Lord draweth nigh.   James 5:7-8 KJV

Be patient, then, brothers and sisters, until the Lord's coming. See how the farmer waits for the land to yield its valuable crop, patiently waiting for the autumn and spring rains. You too, be patient and stand firm, because the Lord's coming is near.   James 5:7-8 NIV

Therefore I will look unto the Lord; I will wait for the God of my salvation: my God will hear me.
                                    Micah 7:7 KJV

But as for me, I watch in hope for the Lord, I wait for God my Savior; my God will hear me.
                                    Micah 7:7 NIV

And so, after he had patiently endured, he obtained the promise.   Hebrews 6:15 KJV

And so after waiting patiently, Abraham received what was promised.   Hebrews 6:15 NIV

He that is slow to wrath is of great understanding: but he that is hasty of spirit exalteth folly.

Proverbs 14:29 KJV

Whoever is patient has great understanding, but one who is quick-tempered displays folly.

Proverbs 14:29 NIV

Be careful for nothing; but in every thing by prayer and supplication with thanksgiving let your requests be made known unto God. Philippians 4:6 KJV

Do not be anxious about anything, but in every situation, by prayer and petition, with thanksgiving, present your requests to God. Philippians 4:6 NIV

Preach the word; be instant in season, out of season; reprove, rebuke, exhort with all long suffering and doctrine. 2 Timothy 4:2 KJV

Preach the word; be prepared in season and out of season; correct, rebuke and encourage—with great patience and careful instruction. 2 Timothy 4:2 NIV

Peace

The Lord bless thee, and keep thee: The Lord make his face shine upon thee, and be gracious unto thee: The Lord lift up his countenance upon thee, and give thee peace.   Numbers 6:24-26 KJV

The Lord bless you and keep you; the Lord make his face shine on you and be gracious to you; the Lord turn his face toward you and give you peace.
                    Numbers 6:24-26 NIV

When a man's ways please the Lord, he maketh even his enemies to be at peace with him.   Proverbs 16:7 KJV

When the Lord takes pleasure in anyone's way, he causes their enemies to make peace with them.
                    Proverbs 16:7 NIV

Acquaint now thyself with him, and be at peace: thereby good shall come unto thee.   Job 22-21 KJV

Submit to God and be at peace with him; in this way prosperity will come to you.   Job 22:21 NIV

Depart from evil, and do good; seek peace, and pursue it. Psalm 34:14 KJV

Turn from evil and do good; seek peace and pursue it. Psalm 34:14 NIV

Great peace have they which love thy law: and nothing shall offend them. Psalm 119:165 KJV

Great peace have those who love your law, and nothing can make them stumble. Psalm 119:165 NIV

And the God of peace shall bruise Satan under your feet shortly. The grace of our Lord Jesus Christ be with you. Amen. Romans 16:20 KJV

The God of peace will soon crush Satan under your feet. The grace of our Lord Jesus be with you. Romans 16:20 NIV

Therefore being justified by faith, we have peace with God through our Lord Jesus Christ. Romans 5:1 KJV

Therefore, since we have been justified through faith, we have peace with God through our Lord Jesus Christ. Romans 5:1 NIV

Praise

Praise ye the Lord. Praise God in his sanctuary: praise him in the firmament of his power. Praise him for his mighty acts: praise him according to his excellent greatness. Praise him with the sound of the trumpet: praise him with the psaltery and harp. Praise him with the timbrel and dance: praise him with stringed instruments and organs. Praise him upon the loud cymbals: praise him upon the high sounding cymbals. Let every thing that hath breath praise the Lord. Praise ye the Lord.   Psalm 150:1-6 KJV

Praise the Lord. Praise God in his sanctuary; praise him in his mighty heavens. Praise him for his acts of power; praise him for his surpassing greatness. Praise him with the sounding of the trumpet, praise him with the harp and lyre, praise him with timbrel and dancing, praise him with the strings and pipe, praise him with the clash of cymbals, praise him with resounding cymbals. Let everything that has breath praise the Lord. Praise the Lord.   Psalm 150:1-6 NIV

By him therefore let us offer the sacrifice of praise to God continually, that is, the fruit of our lips giving thanks to his name.   Hebrews 13:15 KJV

Through Jesus, therefore, let us continually offer to God a sacrifice of praise—the fruit of lips that openly profess his name.   Hebrews 13:15 NIV

Enter into his gates with thanksgiving, and into his courts with praise: be thankful unto him, and bless his name. For the Lord is good; his mercy is everlasting; and his truth endureth to all generations.

Psalm 100:4-5 KJV

Enter his gates with thanksgiving and his courts with praise; give thanks to him and praise his name. For the Lord is good and his love endures forever; his faithfulness continues through all generations.

Psalm 100:4-5 NIV

Is any among you afflicted? let him pray. Is any merry? let him sing psalms.

James 5:13 KJV

Is anyone among you in trouble? Let them pray. Is anyone happy? Let them sing songs of praise.

James 5:13 NIV

But thanks be to God, which giveth us the victory through our Lord Jesus Christ.

1 Corinthians 15:57 KJV

But thanks be to God! He gives us the victory through our Lord Jesus Christ.

1 Corinthians 15:57 NIV

Prayer

After this manner therefore pray ye: Our Father which art in heaven, Hallowed be thy name. Thy kingdom come, Thy will be done in earth, as it is in heaven. Give us this day our daily bread. And forgive us our debts, as we forgive our debtors. And lead us not into temptation, but deliver us from evil: For thine is the kingdom, and the power, and the glory, for ever. Amen.

Matthew 6:9-13 KJV

This, then, is how you should pray: Our Father in heaven, hallowed be your name, your kingdom come, your will be done, on earth as it is in heaven. Give us today our daily bread. And forgive us our debts, as we also have forgiven our debtors. And lead us not into temptation, but deliver us from the evil one.

Matthew 6:9-13 NIV

If my people, which are called by my name, shall humble themselves, and pray, and seek my face, and turn from their wicked ways; then will I hear from heaven, and will forgive their sin, and will heal their land.

2 Chronicles 7:14 KJV

If my people, who are called by my name, will humble themselves and pray and seek my face and turn from their wicked ways, then I will hear from heaven, and I will forgive their sin and will heal their land.

2 Chronicles 7:14 NIV

Likewise the Spirit also helpeth our infirmities: for we know not what we should pray for as we ought: but the Spirit itself maketh intercession for us with groanings which cannot be uttered.   Romans 8:26 KJV

In the same way, the Spirit helps us in our weakness. We do not know what we ought to pray for, but the Spirit himself intercedes for us through wordless groans.
                                                          Romans 8:26 NIV

Confess your faults one to another, and pray one for another, that ye may be healed. The effectual fervent prayer of a righteous man availeth much.
                                                          James 5:16 KJV

Therefore confess your sins to each other and pray for each other so that you may be healed. The prayer of a righteous person is powerful and effective.
                                                          James 5:16 NIV

Therefore I say unto you, What things soever ye desire, when ye pray, believe that ye receive them, and ye shall have them.   Mark 11:24 KJV

Therefore I tell you, whatever you ask for in prayer, believe that you have received it, and it will be yours.
                                                          Mark 11:24 NIV

Protection

The Lord preserveth all them that love him: but all the wicked will he destroy. Psalm 145:20 KJV

The Lord watches over all who love him, but all the wicked he will destroy. Psalm 145:20 NIV

But the Lord is faithful, who shall stablish you, and keep you from evil.

2 Thessalonians 3:3 KJV

But the Lord is faithful, and he will strengthen you and protect you from the evil one.

2 Thessalonians 3:3 NIV

Cast thy burden upon the Lord, and he shall sustain thee: he shall never suffer the righteous to be moved.

Psalm 55:22 KJV

Cast your cares on the Lord and he will sustain you; he will never let the righteous be shaken.

Psalm 55:22 NIV

No weapon that is formed against thee shall prosper; and every tongue that shall rise against thee in judgment thou shalt condemn. This is the heritage of the servants of the Lord, and their righteousness is of me, saith the Lord.

Isaiah 54:17 KJV

No weapon forged against you will prevail, and you will refute every tongue that accuses you. This is the heritage of the servants of the Lord, and this is their vindication from me, declares the Lord.

Isaiah 54:17 NIV

Fear thou not; for I am with thee: be not dismayed; for I am thy God: I will strengthen thee; yea, I will help thee; yea, I will uphold thee with the right hand of my righteousness.

Isaiah 41:10 KJV

So do not fear, for I am with you; do not be dismayed, for I am your God. I will strengthen you and help you; I will uphold you with my righteous right hand.

Isaiah 41:10 NIV

The Lord shall fight for you, and ye shall hold your peace.   Exodus 14:14 KJV

The Lord will fight for you; you need only to be still.

Exodus 14:14 NIV

Purpose

For I know the thoughts that I think toward you, saith the Lord, thoughts of peace, and not of evil, to give you an expected end.   Jeremiah 29:11 KJV

For I know the plans I have for you, declares the Lord, plans to prosper you and not to harm you, plans to give you hope and a future.   Jeremiah 29:11 NIV

And we know that all things work together for good to them that love God, to them who are the called according to his purpose.   Romans 8:28 KJV

And we know that in all things God works for the good of those who love him, who have been called according to his purpose.   Romans 8:28 NIV

For we are his workmanship, created in Christ Jesus unto good works, which God hath before ordained that we should walk in them.   Ephesians 2:10 KJV

For we are God's handiwork, created in Christ Jesus to do good works, which God prepared in advance for us to do.   Ephesians 2:10 NIV

And Jesus came and spake unto them, saying, All power is given unto me in heaven and in earth. Go ye therefore, and teach all nations, baptizing them in the name of the Father, and of the Son, and of the Holy Ghost: Teaching them to observe all things whatsoever I have commanded you: and, lo, I am with you always, even unto the end of the world. Amen. Matthew 28:18-20 KJV

Then Jesus came to them and said, "All authority in heaven and on earth has been given to me. Therefore go and make disciples of all nations, baptizing them in the name of the Father and of the Son and of the Holy Spirit, and teaching them to obey everything I have commanded you. And surely I am with you always, to the very end of the age." Matthew 28:18-20 NIV

For so is the will of God, that with well doing ye may put to silence the ignorance of foolish men.
1 Peter 2:15 KJV

For it is God's will that by doing good you should silence the ignorant talk of foolish people.
1 Peter 2:15 NIV

To every thing there is a season, and a time to every purpose under the heaven. Ecclesiastes 3:1 KJV

There is a time for everything, and a season for every activity under the heavens. Ecclesiastes 3:1 NIV

Rebellions

What? know ye not that your body is the temple of the Holy Ghost which is in you, which ye have of God, and ye are not your own?

1 Corinthians 6:19-20 KJV

Do you not know that your bodies are temples of the Holy Spirit, who is in you, whom you have received from God? You are not your own; you were bought at a price. Therefore honor God with your bodies.

Corinthians 6:19-20 NIV

Likewise, ye younger, submit yourselves unto the elder. Yea, all of you be subject one to another, and be clothed with humility: for God resisteth the proud, and giveth grace to the humble. Humble yourselves therefore under the mighty hand of God, that he may exalt you in due time.

1 Peter 5:5-6 KJV

In the same way, you who are younger, submit yourselves to your elders. All of you, clothe yourselves with humility toward one another, because, God opposes the proud but shows favor to the humble. Humble yourselves, therefore, under God's mighty hand, that he may lift you up in due time.

1 Peter 5:5-6 NIV

Beloved, believe not every spirit, but try the spirits whether they are of God: because many false prophets are gone out into the world. 1 John 4:1 KJV

Dear friends, do not believe every spirit, but test the spirits to see whether they are from God, because many false prophets have gone out into the world.
1 John 4:1 NIV

For rebellion is as the sin of witchcraft, and stubbornness is as iniquity and idolatry. Because thou hast rejected the word of the Lord, he hath also rejected thee from being king. 1 Samuel 15:23 KJV

For rebellion is like the sin of divination, and arrogance like the evil of idolatry. Because you have rejected the word of the Lord, he has rejected you as king.
1 Samuel 15:23 NIV

And he laid hold on the dragon, that old serpent, which is the Devil, and Satan, and bound him a thousand years.
Revelation 20:2 KJV

He seized the dragon, that ancient serpent, who is the devil, or Satan, and bound him for a thousand years.
Revelation 20:2 NIV

Redemption

In whom we have redemption through his blood, the forgiveness of sins, according to the riches of his grace.
Ephesians 1:7 KJV

In him we have redemption through his blood, the forgiveness of sins, in accordance with the riches of God's grace.
Ephesians 1:7 NIV

Christ hath redeemed us from the curse of the law, being made a curse for us: for it is written, Cursed is every one that hangeth on a tree.
Galatians 3:13 KJV

Christ redeemed us from the curse of the law by becoming a curse for us, for it is written: "Cursed is everyone who is hung on a pole."
Galatians 3:13 NIV

I am crucified with Christ: nevertheless I live; yet not I, but Christ liveth in me: and the life which I now live in the flesh I live by the faith of the Son of God, who loved me, and gave himself for me.
Galatians 2:20 KJV

I have been crucified with Christ and I no longer live, but Christ lives in me. The life I now live in the body, I live by faith in the Son of God, who loved me and gave himself for me.
Galatians 2:20 NIV

Forasmuch as ye know that ye were not redeemed with corruptible things, as silver and gold, from your vain conversation received by tradition from your fathers; But with the precious blood of Christ, as of a lamb without blemish and without spot.   1 Peter 1:18-19 KJV

For you know that it was not with perishable things such as silver or gold that you were redeemed from the empty way of life handed down to you from your ancestors, but with the precious blood of Christ, a lamb without blemish or defect.   1 Peter 1:18-19 NIV

Who hath delivered us from the power of darkness, and hath translated us into the kingdom of his dear Son: In whom we have redemption through his blood, even the forgiveness of sins.   Colossians 1:13-14 KJV

For he has rescued us from the dominion of darkness and brought us into the kingdom of the Son he loves, in whom we have redemption, the forgiveness of sins.
    Colossians 1:13-14 NIV

For ye are bought with a price: therefore glorify God in your body, and in your spirit, which are God's.
    1 Corinthians 6:20 KJV

You were bought at a price. Therefore honor God with your bodies.   1 Corinthians 6:20 NIV

Repentance

If my people, which are called by my name, shall humble themselves, and pray, and seek my face, and turn from their wicked ways; then will I hear from heaven, and will forgive their sin, and will heal their land.

2 Chronicles 7:14 KJV

If my people, who are called by my name, will humble themselves and pray and seek my face and turn from their wicked ways, then I will hear from heaven, and I will forgive their sin and will heal their land.

2 Chronicles 7:14 NIV

From that time Jesus began to preach, and to say, Repent: for the kingdom of heaven is at hand.

Matthew 4:17 KJV

From that time on Jesus began to preach, "Repent, for the kingdom of heaven has come near."

Matthew 4:17 NIV

Bring forth therefore fruits meet for repentance.

Matthew 3:8 KJV

Produce fruit in keeping with repentance.

Matthew 3:8 NIV

I say unto you, that likewise joy shall be in heaven over one sinner that repenteth, more than over ninety and nine just persons, which need no repentance.

Luke 15:7 KJV

I tell you that in the same way there will be more rejoicing in heaven over one sinner who repents than over ninety-nine righteous persons who do not need to repent.

Luke 15:7 NIV

But if the wicked will turn from all his sins that he hath committed, and keep all my statutes, and do that which is lawful and right, he shall surely live, he shall not die.

Ezekiel 18:21 KJV

But if a wicked person turns away from all the sins they have committed and keeps all my decrees and does what is just and right, that person will surely live; they will not die.

Ezekiel 18:21 NIV

In those days came John the Baptist, preaching in the wilderness of Judaea, And saying, Repent ye: for the kingdom of heaven is at hand.

Matthew 3:1-2 KJV

In those days John the Baptist came, preaching in the wilderness of Judea and saying, "Repent, for the kingdom of heaven has come near."

Matthew 3:1-2 NIV

Rest

And on the seventh day God ended his work which he had made; and he rested on the seventh day from all his work which he had made. And God blessed the seventh day, and sanctified it: because that in it he had rested from all his work which God created and made.

Genesis 2:2-3 KJV

By the seventh day God had finished the work he had been doing; so on the seventh day he rested from all his work. Then God blessed the seventh day and made it holy, because on it he rested from all the work of creating that he had done.

Genesis 2:2-3 NIV

Truly my soul waiteth upon God: from him cometh my salvation. He only is my rock and my salvation; he is my defence; I shall not be greatly moved.

Psalm 62:1-2 KJV

Truly my soul finds rest in God; my salvation comes from him. Truly he is my rock and my salvation; he is my fortress, I will never be shaken.

Psalm 62:1-2 NIV

Rest in the Lord, and wait patiently for him: fret not thyself because of him who prospereth in his way, because of the man who bringeth wicked devices to pass.   Psalm 37:7 KJV

Be still before the Lord and wait patiently for him; do not fret when people succeed in their ways, when they carry out their wicked schemes.   Psalm 37:7 NIV

Come unto me, all ye that labour and are heavy laden, and I will give you rest. Take my yoke upon you, and learn of me; for I am meek and lowly in heart: and ye shall find rest unto your souls.   Matthew 11:28-29 KJV

Come to me, all you who are weary and burdened, and I will give you rest. Take my yoke upon you and learn from me, for I am gentle and humble in heart, and you will find rest for your souls.   Matthew 11:28-29 NIV

I am the Lord your God; walk in my statutes, and keep my judgments, and do them; And hallow my sabbaths; and they shall be a sign between me and you, that ye may know that I am the Lord your God.
                                              Ezekiel 20:19-20 KJV

I am the Lord your God; follow my decrees and be careful to keep my laws. Keep my Sabbaths holy, that they may be a sign between us. Then you will know that I am the Lord your God.   Ezekiel 20:19-20 NIV

Righteousness

Sow to yourselves in righteousness, reap in mercy; break up your fallow ground: for it is time to seek the Lord, till he come and rain righteousness upon you.

Hosea 10:12 KJV

Sow righteousness for yourselves, reap the fruit of unfailing love, and break up your unplowed ground; for it is time to seek the Lord, until he comes and showers his righteousness on you.

Hosea 10:12 NIV

Blessed are they which do hunger and thirst after righteousness: for they shall be filled.

Matthew 5:6 KJV

Blessed are those who hunger and thirst for righteousness, for they will be filled.

Matthew 5:6 NIV

And the work of righteousness shall be peace; and the effect of righteousness quietness and assurance for ever.

Isaiah 32:17 KJV

The fruit of that righteousness will be peace; its effect will be quietness and confidence forever.

Isaiah 32:17 NIV

For the eyes of the Lord are over the righteous, and his ears are open unto their prayers: but the face of the Lord is against them that do evil.

1 Peter 3:12 KJV

For the eyes of the Lord are on the righteous and his ears are attentive to their prayer, but the face of the Lord is against those who do evil.

1 Peter 3:12 NIV

Surely he shall not be moved for ever: the righteous shall be in everlasting remembrance. He shall not be afraid of evil tidings: his heart is fixed, trusting in the Lord.

Psalm 112:6-7 KJV

Surely the righteous will never be shaken; they will be remembered forever. They will have no fear of bad news; their hearts are steadfast, trusting in the Lord.

Psalm 112:6-7 NIV

The mouth of the righteous speaketh wisdom, and his tongue talketh of judgment. The law of his God is in his heart; none of his steps shall slide.

Psalm 37:30-31 KJV

The mouths of the righteous utter wisdom, and their tongues speak what is just. The law of their God is in their hearts; their feet do not slip.

Psalm 37:30-31 NIV

Salvation

That if thou shalt confess with thy mouth the Lord Jesus, and shalt believe in thine heart that God hath raised him from the dead, thou shalt be saved.

Romans 10:9 KJV

If you declare with your mouth, "Jesus is Lord," and believe in your heart that God raised him from the dead, you will be saved.

Romans 10:9 NIV

If we confess our sins, he is faithful and just to forgive us our sins, and to cleanse us from all unrighteousness.

1 John 1:9 KJV

If we confess our sins, he is faithful and just and will forgive us our sins and purify us from all unrighteousness.

1 John 1:9 NIV

Jesus answered and said unto him, Verily, verily, I say unto thee, Except a man be born again, he cannot see the kingdom of God.

John 3:3 KJV

Jesus replied, "Very truly I tell you, no one can see the kingdom of God unless they are born again."

John 3:3 NIV

For God so loved the world, that he gave his only begotten Son, that whosoever believeth in him should not perish, but have everlasting life. For God sent not his Son into the world to condemn the world; but that the world through him might be saved.   John 3:16-17 KJV

For God so loved the world that he gave his one and only Son, that whoever believes in him shall not perish but have eternal life. For God did not send his Son into the world to condemn the world, but to save the world through him.   John 3:16-17 NIV

For by grace are ye saved through faith; and that not of yourselves: it is the gift of God: Not of works, lest any man should boast.   Ephesians 2:8-9 KJV

For it is by grace you have been saved, through faith and this is not from yourselves, it is the gift of God not by works, so that no one can boast.   Ephesians 2:8-9 NIV

To him give all the prophets witness, that through his name whosoever believeth in him shall receive remission of sins.   Acts 10:43 KJV

All the prophets testify about him that everyone who believes in him receives forgiveness of sins through his name.   Acts 10:43 NIV

Satan

For we wrestle not against flesh and blood, but against principalities, against powers, against the rulers of the darkness of this world, against spiritual wickedness in high places.   Ephesians 6:12 KJV

For our struggle is not against flesh and blood, but against the rulers, against the authorities, against the powers of this dark world and against the spiritual forces of evil in the heavenly realms.   Ephesians 6:12 NIV

Forasmuch then as the children are partakers of flesh and blood, he also himself likewise took part of the same; that through death he might destroy him that had the power of death, that is, the devil.   Hebrews 2:14 KJV

Since the children have flesh and blood, he too shared in their humanity so that by his death he might break the power of him who holds the power of death—that is, the devil.   Hebrews 2:14 NIV

Be sober, be vigilant; because your adversary the devil, as a roaring lion, walketh about, seeking whom he may devour.   1 Peter 5:8 KJV

Be alert and of sober mind. Your enemy the devil prowls around like a roaring lion looking for someone to devour.   1 Peter 5:8 NIV

He that committeth sin is of the devil; for the devil sinneth from the beginning. For this purpose the Son of God was manifested, that he might destroy the works of the devil. 1 John 3:8 KJV

The one who does what is sinful is of the devil, because the devil has been sinning from the beginning. The reason the Son of God appeared was to destroy the devil's work. 1 John 3:8 NIV

And no marvel; for Satan himself is transformed into an angel of light. Therefore it is no great thing if his ministers also be transformed as the ministers of righteousness; whose end shall be according to their works. 2 Corinthians 11:14-15 KJV

And no wonder, for Satan himself masquerades as an angel of light. It is not surprising, then, if his servants also masquerade as servants of righteousness. Their end will be what their actions deserve.
2 Corinthians 11:14-15 NIV

And the God of peace shall bruise Satan under your feet shortly. The grace of our Lord Jesus Christ be with you. Amen. Romans 16:20 KJV

The God of peace will soon crush Satan under your feet. The grace of our Lord Jesus be with you.
Romans 16:20 NIV

Scripture

For whatsoever things were written aforetime were written for our learning, that we through patience and comfort of the scriptures might have hope.

Romans 15:4 KJV

For everything that was written in the past was written to teach us, so that through the endurance taught in the Scriptures and the encouragement they provide we might have hope.

Romans 15:4 NIV

All scripture is given by inspiration of God, and is profitable for doctrine, for reproof, for correction, for instruction in righteousness.

2 Timothy 3:16 KJV

All Scripture is God-breathed and is useful for teaching, rebuking, correcting and training in righteousness.

2 Timothy 3:16 NIV

But he answered and said, It is written, Man shall not live by bread alone, but by every word that proceedeth out of the mouth of God.

Matthew 4:4 KJV

Jesus answered, "It is written: 'Man shall not live on bread alone, but on every word that comes from the mouth of God.'"

Matthew 4:4 NIV

For the word of God is quick, and powerful, and sharper than any twoedged sword, piercing even to the dividing asunder of soul and spirit, and of the joints and marrow, and is a discerner of the thoughts and intents of the heart.   Hebrews 4:12 KJV

For the word of God is alive and active. Sharper than any double-edged sword, it penetrates even to dividing soul and spirit, joints and marrow; it judges the thoughts and attitudes of the heart.   Hebrews 4:12 NIV

Heaven and earth shall pass away, but my words shall not pass away.   Matthew 24:35 KJV

Heaven and earth will pass away, but my words will never pass away.   Matthew 24:35 NIV

This book of the law shall not depart out of thy mouth; but thou shalt meditate therein day and night, that thou mayest observe to do according to all that is written therein: for then thou shalt make thy way prosperous, and then thou shalt have good success.
                                                    Joshua 1:8 KJV

Keep this Book of the Law always on your lips; meditate on it day and night, so that you may be careful to do everything written in it. Then you will be prosperous and successful.
                                                    Joshua 1:8 NIV

I have set the Lord always before me: because he is at my right hand, I shall not be moved.

Psalm 16:8 KJV

I keep my eyes always on the Lord. With him at my right hand, I will not be shaken.

Psalm 16:8 NIV

Behold, I will bring it health and cure, and I will cure them, and will reveal unto them the abundance of peace and truth.

Jeremiah 33:6 KJV

Nevertheless, I will bring health and healing to it; I will heal my people and will let them enjoy abundant peace and security.

Jeremiah 33:6 NIV

God is our refuge and strength, a very present help in trouble.

Psalm 46:1 KJV

God is our refuge and strength, an ever-present help in trouble.

Psalm 46:1 NIV

Surely he shall deliver thee from the snare of the fowler, and from the noisome pestilence. He shall cover thee with his feathers, and under his wings shalt thou trust: his truth shall be thy shield and buckler.

Psalm 91:3-4 KJV

Surely he will save you from the fowler's snare and from the deadly pestilence. He will cover you with his feathers, and under his wings you will find refuge; his faithfulness will be your shield and rampart.

Psalm 91:3-4 NIV

Because thou hast made the Lord, which is my refuge, even the most High, thy habitation; There shall no evil befall thee, neither shall any plague come nigh thy dwelling. For he shall give his angels charge over thee, to keep thee in all thy ways.   Psalm 91:9-11 KJV

If you say, "The Lord is my refuge," and you make the Most High your dwelling, no harm will overtake you, no disaster will come near your tent. For he will command his angels concerning you to guard you in all your ways.

Psalm 91:9-11 NIV

Peace be within thy walls, and prosperity within thy palaces.   Psalm 122:7 KJV

May there be peace within your walls and security within your citadels.   Psalm 122:7 NIV

Self-Worth

Before I formed thee in the belly I knew thee; and before thou camest forth out of the womb I sanctified thee, and I ordained thee a prophet unto the nations.

Jeremiah 1:5 KJV

"Before I formed you in the womb I knew you, before you were born I set you apart; I appointed you as a prophet to the nations." Jeremiah 1:5 NIV

Are not two sparrows sold for a farthing? and one of them shall not fall on the ground without your Father. But the very hairs of your head are all numbered. Fear ye not therefore, ye are of more value than many sparrows. Matthew 10:29-31 KJV

Are not two sparrows sold for a penny? Yet not one of them will fall to the ground outside your Father's care. And even the very hairs of your head are all numbered. So don't be afraid; you are worth more than many sparrows. Matthew 10:29-31 NIV

Seest thou a man wise in his own conceit? there is more hope of a fool than of him. Proverbs 26:12 KJV

Do you see a person wise in their own eyes? There is more hope for a fool than for them. Proverbs 26:12 NIV

Know ye that the Lord he is God: it is he that hath made us, and not we ourselves; we are his people, and the sheep of his pasture.   Psalm 100:3 KJV

Know that the Lord is God. It is he who made us, and we are his; we are his people, the sheep of his pasture.
                                        Psalm 100:3 NIV

For thou hast possessed my reins: thou hast covered me in my mother's womb. I will praise thee; for I am fearfully and wonderfully made: marvellous are thy works; and that my soul knoweth right well.
                                    Psalm 139:13-14 KJV

For you created my inmost being; you knit me together in my mother's womb. I praise you because I am fearfully and wonderfully made; your works are wonderful, I know that full well.
                                    Psalm 139:13-14 NIV

For all have sinned, and come short of the glory of God.
                                        Romans 3:23 KJV

For all have sinned and fall short of the glory of God.
                                        Romans 3:23 NIV

Serving

If any man serve me, let him follow me; and where I am, there shall also my servant be: if any man serve me, him will my Father honour.   John 12:26 KJV

Whoever serves me must follow me; and where I am, my servant also will be. My Father will honor the one who serves me.   John 12:26 NIV

For even the Son of man came not to be ministered unto, but to minister, and to give his life a ransom for many.   Mark 10:45 KJV

For even the Son of Man did not come to be served, but to serve, and to give his life as a ransom for many.   Mark 10:45 NIV

Not slothful in business; fervent in spirit; serving the Lord.   Romans 12:11 KJV

Never be lacking in zeal, but keep your spiritual fervor, serving the Lord.   Romans 12:11 NIV

And if it seem evil unto you to serve the Lord, choose you this day whom ye will serve; whether the gods which your fathers served that were on the other side of the flood, or the gods of the Amorites, in whose land ye dwell: but as for me and my house, we will serve the Lord.   Joshua 24:15 KJV

But if serving the Lord seems undesirable to you, then choose for yourselves this day whom you will serve, whether the gods your ancestors served beyond the Euphrates, or the gods of the Amorites, in whose land you are living. But as for me and my household, we will serve the Lord.   Joshua 24:15 NIV

As every man hath received the gift, even so minister the same one to another, as good stewards of the manifold grace of God.   1 Peter 4:10 KJV

Each of you should use whatever gift you have received to serve others, as faithful stewards of God's grace in its various forms.   1 Peter 4:10 NIV

As we have therefore opportunity, let us do good unto all men, especially unto them who are of the household of faith.   Galatians 6:10 KJV

Therefore, as we have opportunity, let us do good to all people, especially to those who belong to the family of believers.   Galatians 6:10 NIV

Singleness

I say therefore to the unmarried and widows, it is good for them if they abide even as I. But if they cannot contain, let them marry: for it is better to marry than to burn.   1 Corinthians 7:8-9 KJV

Now to the unmarried and the widows I say: It is good for them to stay unmarried, as I do. But if they cannot control themselves, they should marry, for it is better to marry than to burn with passion.   1 Corinthians 7:8-9 NIV

Flee fornication. Every sin that a man doeth is without the body; but he that committeth fornication sinneth against his own body. What? know ye not that your body is the temple of the Holy Ghost which is in you, which ye have of God, and ye are not your own? For ye are bought with a price: therefore glorify God in your body, and in your spirit, which are God's.
                                   1 Corinthians 6:18-20 KJV

Flee from sexual immorality. All other sins a person commits are outside the body, but whoever sins sexually, sins against their own body. Do you not know that your bodies are temples of the Holy Spirit, who is in you, whom you have received from God? You are not your own; you were bought at a price. Therefore honor God with your bodies.   1 Corinthians 6:18-20 NIV

But I would have you without carefulness. He that is unmarried careth for the things that belong to the Lord, how he may please the Lord: But he that is married careth for the things that are of the world, how he may please his wife.   1 Corinthians 7:32-33 KJV

I would like you to be free from concern. An unmarried man is concerned about the Lord's affairs—how he can please the Lord. But a married man is concerned about the affairs of this world—how he can please his wife.
1 Corinthians 7:32-33 NIV

There is difference also between a wife and a virgin. The unmarried woman careth for the things of the Lord, that she may be holy both in body and in spirit: but she that is married careth for the things of the world, how she may please her husband. And this I speak for your own profit; not that I may cast a snare upon you, but for that which is comely, and that ye may attend upon the Lord without distraction.   1 Corinthians 7:34-35 KJV

And his interests are divided. An unmarried woman or virgin is concerned about the Lord's affairs: Her aim is to be devoted to the Lord in both body and spirit. But a married woman is concerned about the affairs of this world—how she can please her husband. I am saying this for your own good, not to restrict you, but that you may live in a right way in undivided devotion to the Lord.   1 Corinthians 7:34-35 NIV

Stability

The steps of a good man are ordered by the Lord: and he delighteth in his way. Though he fall, he shall not be utterly cast down: for the Lord upholdeth him with his hand.   Psalm 37:23-24 KJV

The Lord makes firm the steps of the one who delights in him; though he may stumble, he will not fall, for the Lord upholds him with his hand.   Psalm 37:23-24 NIV

He that walketh uprightly walketh surely: but he that perverteth his ways shall be known.

Proverbs 10:9 KJV

Whoever walks in integrity walks securely, but whoever takes crooked paths will be found out.

Proverbs 10:9 NIV

He that loveth his brother abideth in the light, and there is none occasion of stumbling in him.

1 John 2:10 KJV

Anyone who loves their brother and sister lives in the light, and there is nothing in them to make them stumble.

1 John 2:10 NIV

I have set the Lord always before me: because he is at my right hand, I shall not be moved.

Psalm 16:8 KJV

I keep my eyes always on the Lord. With him at my right hand, I will not be shaken.

Psalm 16:8 NIV

For thou hast delivered my soul from death, mine eyes from tears, and my feet from falling. I will walk before the Lord in the land of the living.

Psalm 116:8-9 KJV

For you, Lord, have delivered me from death, my eyes from tears, my feet from stumbling, that I may walk before the Lord in the land of the living.

Psalm 116:8-9 NIV

He brought me up also out of an horrible pit, out of the miry clay, and set my feet upon a rock, and established my goings.

Psalm 40:2 KJV

He lifted me out of the slimy pit, out of the mud and mire; he set my feet on a rock and gave me a firm place to stand.

Psalm 40:2 NIV

Stewardship

As every man hath received the gift, even so minister the same one to another, as good stewards of the manifold grace of God.   1 Peter 4:10 KJV

Each of you should use whatever gift you have received to serve others, as faithful stewards of God's grace in its various forms.   1 Peter 4:10 NIV

But this I say, He which soweth sparingly shall reap also sparingly; and he which soweth bountifully shall reap also bountifully. Every man according as he purposeth in his heart, so let him give; not grudgingly, or of necessity: for God loveth a cheerful giver.
                                    2 Corinthians 9:6-7 KJV

Remember this: Whoever sows sparingly will also reap sparingly, and whoever sows generously will also reap generously. Each of you should give what you have decided in your heart to give, not reluctantly or under compulsion, for God loves a cheerful giver.
                                    2 Corinthians 9:6-7 NIV

Commit thy works unto the Lord, and thy thoughts shall be established.   Proverbs 16:3 KJV

Commit to the Lord whatever you do, and he will establish your plans.   Proverbs 16:3 NIV

And God blessed them, and God said unto them, Be fruitful, and multiply, and replenish the earth, and subdue it: and have dominion over the fish of the sea, and over the fowl of the air, and over every living thing that moveth upon the earth. Genesis 1:28 KJV

God blessed them and said to them, "Be fruitful and increase in number; fill the earth and subdue it. Rule over the fish in the sea and the birds in the sky and over every living creature that moves on the ground."
Genesis 1:28 NIV

And whatsoever ye do, do it heartily, as to the Lord, and not unto men; Knowing that of the Lord ye shall receive the reward of the inheritance: for ye serve the Lord Christ. Colossians 3:23-24 KJV

Whatever you do, work at it with all your heart, as working for the Lord, not for human masters, since you know that you will receive an inheritance from the Lord as a reward. It is the Lord Christ you are serving.
Colossians 3:23-24 NIV

Honour the Lord with thy substance, and with the firstfruits of all thine increase. Proverbs 3:9 KJV

Honor the Lord with your wealth, with the firstfruits of all your crops. Proverbs 3:9 NIV

Strength

I can do all things through Christ which strengthens me.

Philippians 4:13 KJV

I can do all this through him who gives me strength.

Philippians 4:13 NIV

Fear thou not; for I am with thee: be not dismayed; for I am thy God: I will strengthen thee; yea, I will help thee; yea, I will uphold thee with the right hand of my righteousness.   Isaiah 41:10 KJV

So do not fear, for I am with you; do not be dismayed, for I am your God. I will strengthen you and help you; I will uphold you with my righteous right hand.

Isaiah 41:10 NIV

God is my strength and power: and he maketh my way perfect. He maketh my feet like hinds' feet: and setteth me upon my high places.

2 Samuel 22:33-34 KJV

It is God who arms me with strength and keeps my way secure. He makes my feet like the feet of a deer; he causes me to stand on the heights.

2 Samuel 22:33-34 NIV

But they that wait upon the Lord shall renew their strength; they shall mount up with wings as eagles; they shall run, and not be weary; and they shall walk, and not faint.
Isaiah 40:31 KJV

But those who hope in the Lord will renew their strength. They will soar on wings like eagles; they will run and not grow weary, they will walk and not be faint.
Isaiah 40:31 NIV

The Lord is my strength and song, and he is become my salvation: he is my God, and I will prepare him an habitation; my father's God, and I will exalt him.
Exodus 15:2 KJV

The Lord is my strength and my defense; he has become my salvation. He is my God, and I will praise him, my father's God, and I will exalt him.
Exodus 15:2 NIV

Seek the Lord and his strength, seek his face continually.
1 Chronicles 16:11 KJV

Look to the Lord and his strength; seek his face always.
1 Chronicles 16:11 NIV

Temptation

There hath no temptation taken you but such as is common to man: but God is faithful, who will not suffer you to be tempted above that ye are able; but will with the temptation also make a way to escape, that ye may be able to bear it. 1 Corinthians 10:13 KJV

No temptation has overtaken you except what is common to mankind. And God is faithful; he will not let you be tempted beyond what you can bear. But when you are tempted, he will also provide a way out so that you can endure it. 1 Corinthians 10:13 NIV

If we confess our sins, he is faithful and just to forgive us our sins, and to cleanse us from all unrighteousness. 1 John 1:9 KJV

If we confess our sins, he is faithful and just and will forgive us our sins and purify us from all unrighteousness. 1 John 1:9 NIV

Submit yourselves therefore to God. Resist the devil, and he will flee from you. James 4:7 KJV

Submit yourselves, then, to God. Resist the devil, and he will flee from you. James 4:7 NIV

Finally, my brethren, be strong in the Lord, and in the power of his might. Put on the whole armour of God, that ye may be able to stand against the wiles of the devil.

Ephesians 6:10-11 KJV

Finally, be strong in the Lord and in his mighty power. Put on the full armor of God, so that you can take your stand against the devil's schemes.

Ephesians 6:10-11 NIV

Blessed is the man that endureth temptation: for when he is tried, he shall receive the crown of life, which the Lord hath promised to them that love him.

James 1:12 KJV

Blessed is the one who perseveres under trial because, having stood the test, that person will receive the crown of life that the Lord has promised to those who love him.

James 1:12 NIV

For sin shall not have dominion over you: for ye are not under the law, but under grace.

Romans 6:14 KJV

For sin shall no longer be your master, because you are not under the law, but under grace.

Romans 6:14 NIV

Thankfulness

Let the word of Christ dwell in you richly in all wisdom; teaching and admonishing one another in psalms and hymns and spiritual songs, singing with grace in your hearts to the Lord. And whatsoever ye do in word or deed, do all in the name of the Lord Jesus, giving thanks to God and the Father by him.

Colossians 3:16-17 KJV

Let the message of Christ dwell among you richly as you teach and admonish one another with all wisdom through psalms, hymns, and songs from the Spirit, singing to God with gratitude in your hearts. And whatever you do, whether in word or deed, do it all in the name of the Lord Jesus, giving thanks to God the Father through him.

Colossians 3:16-17 NIV

Enter into his gates with thanksgiving, and into his courts with praise: be thankful unto him, and bless his name.

Psalm 100:4 KJV

Enter his gates with thanksgiving and his courts with praise; give thanks to him and praise his name.

Psalm 100:4 NIV

In every thing give thanks: for this is the will of God in Christ Jesus concerning you.

1 Thessalonians 5:18 KJV

Give thanks in all circumstances; for this is God's will for you in Christ Jesus.

1 Thessalonians 5:18 NIV

Be careful for nothing; but in every thing by prayer and supplication with thanksgiving let your requests be made known unto God.

Philippians 4:6 KJV

Do not be anxious about anything, but in every situation, by prayer and petition, with thanksgiving, present your requests to God.

Philippians 4:6 NIV

Oh that men would praise the Lord for his goodness, and for his wonderful works to the children of men! For he satisfieth the longing soul, and filleth the hungry soul with goodness.

Psalm 107:8-9 KJV

Let them give thanks to the Lord for his unfailing love and his wonderful deeds for mankind, for he satisfies the thirsty and fills the hungry with good things.

Psalm 107:8-9 NIV

Thoughts

Let the wicked forsake his way, and the unrighteous man his thoughts: and let him return unto the Lord, and he will have mercy upon him; and to our God, for he will abundantly pardon.

Isaiah 55:7 KJV

Let the wicked forsake their ways and the unrighteous their thoughts. Let them turn to the Lord, and he will have mercy on them, and to our God, for he will freely pardon.

Isaiah 55:7 NIV

The Lord knoweth the thoughts of man, that they are vanity. Psalm 94:11 KJV

The Lord knows all human plans; he knows that they are futile. Psalm 94:11 NIV

For to be carnally minded is death; but to be spiritually minded is life and peace.

Romans 8:6 KJV

The mind governed by the flesh is death, but the mind governed by the Spirit is life and peace.

Romans 8:6 NIV

Finally, brethren, whatsoever things are true, whatsoever things are honest, whatsoever things are just, whatsoever things are pure, whatsoever things are lovely, whatsoever things are of good report; if there be any virtue, and if there be any praise, think on these things.

Philippians 4:8 KJV

Finally, brothers and sisters, whatever is true, whatever is noble, whatever is right, whatever is pure, whatever is lovely, whatever is admirable—if anything is excellent or praiseworthy—think about such things.

Philippians 4:8 NIV

And be not conformed to this world: but be ye transformed by the renewing of your mind, that ye may prove what is that good, and acceptable, and perfect, will of God.

Romans 12:2 KJV

Do not conform to the pattern of this world, but be transformed by the renewing of your mind. Then you will be able to test and approve what God's will is—his good, pleasing and perfect will.

Romans 12:2 NIV

Set your affection on things above, not on things on the earth.

Colossians 3:2 KJV

Set your minds on things above, not on earthly things.

Colossians 3:2 NIV

Trouble

The Lord is good, a strong hold in the day of trouble; and he knoweth them that trust in him.

Nahum 1:7 KJV

The Lord is good, a refuge in times of trouble. He cares for those who trust in him.

Nahum 1:7 NIV

These things I have spoken unto you, that in me ye might have peace. In the world ye shall have tribulation: but be of good cheer; I have overcome the world.

John 16:33 KJV

I have told you these things, so that in me you may have peace. In this world you will have trouble. But take heart! I have overcome the world.   John 16:33 NIV

Trouble and anguish have taken hold on me: yet thy commandments are my delights.

Psalm 119:143 KJV

Trouble and distress have come upon me, but your commands give me delight.

Psalm 119:143 NIV

Be strong and of a good courage, fear not, nor be afraid of them: for the Lord thy God, he it is that doth go with thee; he will not fail thee, nor forsake thee.

Deuteronomy 31:6 KJV

Be strong and courageous. Do not be afraid or terrified because of them, for the Lord your God goes with you; he will never leave you nor forsake you.

Deuteronomy 31:6 NIV

Peace I leave with you, my peace I give unto you: not as the world giveth, give I unto you. Let not your heart be troubled, neither let it be afraid.

John 14:27 KJV

Peace I leave with you; my peace I give you. I do not give to you as the world gives. Do not let your hearts be troubled and do not be afraid.

John 14:27 NIV

Wait on the Lord: be of good courage, and he shall strengthen thine heart: wait, I say, on the Lord.

Psalm 27:14 KJV

Wait for the Lord; be strong and take heart and wait for the Lord.

Psalm 27:14 NIV

Trust

It is better to trust in the Lord than to put confidence in man.
Psalm 118:8 KJV

It is better to take refuge in the Lord than to trust in humans.
Psalm 118:8 NIV

Trust in the Lord with all thine heart; and lean not unto thine own understanding. In all thy ways acknowledge him, and he shall direct thy paths.
Proverbs 3:5-6 KJV

Trust in the Lord with all your heart and lean not on your own understanding; in all your ways submit to him, and he will make your paths straight.
Proverbs 3:5-6 NIV

Commit thy way unto the Lord; trust also in him; and he shall bring it to pass.
Psalm 37:5 KJV

Commit your way to the Lord; trust in him and he will do this.
Psalm 37:5 NIV

Blessed is the man that trusteth in the Lord, and whose hope the Lord is. For he shall be as a tree planted by the waters, and that spreadeth out her roots by the river, and shall not see when heat cometh, but her leaf shall be green; and shall not be careful in the year of drought, neither shall cease from yielding fruit.

Jeremiah 17:7-8 KJV

But blessed is the one who trusts in the Lord, whose confidence is in him. They will be like a tree planted by the water that sends out its roots by the stream. It does not fear when heat comes; its leaves are always green. It has no worries in a year of drought and never fails to bear fruit.

Jeremiah 17:7-8 NIV

Let not your heart be troubled: ye believe in God, believe also in me.   John 14:1 KJV

"Do not let your hearts be troubled. You believe in God; believe also in me."   John 14:1 NIV

But I trusted in thee, O Lord: I said, Thou art my God.

Psalm 31:14 KJV

But I trust in you, Lord; I say, "You are my God."

Psalm 31:14 NIV

Truth

Then said Jesus to those Jews which believed on him, If ye continue in my word, then are ye my disciples indeed; And ye shall know the truth, and the truth shall make you free.   John 8:31-32 KJV

To the Jews who had believed him, Jesus said, "If you hold to my teaching, you are really my disciples. Then you will know the truth, and the truth will set you free."
John 8:31-32 NIV

The Lord is nigh unto all them that call upon him, to all that call upon him in truth.   Psalm 145:18 KJV

The Lord is near to all who call on him, to all who call on him in truth.   Psalm 145:18 NIV

Jesus saith unto him, I am the way, the truth, and the life: no man cometh unto the Father, but by me.
John 14:6 KJV

Jesus answered, "I am the way and the truth and the life. No one comes to the Father except through me."
John 14:6 NIV

Howbeit when he, the Spirit of truth, is come, he will guide you into all truth: for he shall not speak of himself; but whatsoever he shall hear, that shall he speak: and he will shew you things to come.

John 16:13 KJV

But when he, the Spirit of truth, comes, he will guide you into all the truth. He will not speak on his own; he will speak only what he hears, and he will tell you what is yet to come.

John 16:13 NIV

Lying lips are abomination to the Lord: but they that deal truly are his delight.

Proverbs 12:22 KJV

The Lord detests lying lips, but he delights in people who are trustworthy.

Proverbs 12:22 NIV

My little children, let us not love in word, neither in tongue; but in deed and in truth.

1 John 3:18 KJV

Dear children, let us not love with words or speech but with actions and in truth.

1 John 3:18 NIV

Unsaved

For God so loved the world, that he gave his only begotten Son, that whosoever believeth in him should not perish, but have everlasting life.

John 3:16 KJV

For God so loved the world that he gave his one and only Son, that whoever believes in him shall not perish but have eternal life.

John 3:16 NIV

For the wages of sin is death; but the gift of God is eternal life through Jesus Christ our Lord.

Romans 6:23 KJV

For the wages of sin is death, but the gift of God is eternal life in Christ Jesus our Lord.

Romans 6:23 NIV

But God commendeth his love toward us, in that, while we were yet sinners, Christ died for us.

Romans 5:8 KJV

But God demonstrates his own love for us in this: While we were still sinners, Christ died for us.

Romans 5:8 NIV

Jesus answered and said unto him, Verily, verily, I say unto thee, Except a man be born again, he cannot see the kingdom of God.

Jesus replied, "Very truly I tell you, no one can see the kingdom of God unless they are born again."

John 3:3 NIV

And he said unto them, Go ye into all the world, and preach the gospel to every creature. He that believeth and is baptized shall be saved; but he that believeth not shall be damned.

Mark 16:15-16 KJV

He said to them, "Go into all the world and preach the gospel to all creation. Whoever believes and is baptized will be saved, but whoever does not believe will be condemned."

Mark 16:15-16 NIV

For God sent not his Son into the world to condemn the world; but that the world through him might be saved.

John 3:17 KJV

For God did not send his Son into the world to condemn the world, but to save the world through him.

John 3:17 NIV

143

Victory

These things I have spoken unto you, that in me ye might have peace. In the world ye shall have tribulation: but be of good cheer; I have overcome the world.

John 16:33 KJV

I have told you these things, so that in me you may have peace. In this world you will have trouble. But take heart! I have overcome the world.

John 16:33 NIV

But thanks be to God, which giveth us the victory through our Lord Jesus Christ.

1 Corinthians 15:57 KJV

But thanks be to God! He gives us the victory through our Lord Jesus Christ.

1 Corinthians 15:57 NIV

Wherefore take unto you the whole armour of God, that ye may be able to withstand in the evil day, and having done all, to stand.

Ephesians 6:13 KJV

Therefore put on the full armor of God, so that when the day of evil comes, you may be able to stand your ground, and after you have done everything, to stand.

Ephesians 6:13 NIV

Ye are of God, little children, and have overcome them: because greater is he that is in you, than he that is in the world.

1 John 4:4 KJV

You, dear children, are from God and have overcome them, because the one who is in you is greater than the one who is in the world.

1 John 4:4 NIV

There is no wisdom nor understanding nor counsel against the Lord. The horse is prepared against the day of battle: but safety is of the Lord.

Proverbs 21:30-31 KJV

There is no wisdom, no insight, no plan that can succeed against the Lord. The horse is made ready for the day of battle, but victory rests with the Lord.

Proverbs 21:30-31 NIV

For the Lord your God is he that goeth with you, to fight for you against your enemies, to save you.

Deuteronomy 20:4 KJV

For the Lord your God is the one who goes with you to fight for you against your enemies to give you victory.

Deuteronomy 20:4 NIV

Wisdom

If any of you lack wisdom, let him ask of God, that giveth to all men liberally, and upbraideth not; and it shall be given him.
James 1:5 KJV

If any of you lacks wisdom, you should ask God, who gives generously to all without finding fault, and it will be given to you.
James 1:5 NIV

The fear of the Lord is the beginning of knowledge: but fools despise wisdom and instruction.
Proverbs 1:7 KJV

The fear of the Lord is the beginning of knowledge, but fools despise wisdom and instruction.
Proverbs 1:7 NIV

Who is a wise man and endued with knowledge among you? let him shew out of a good conversation his works with meekness of wisdom.
James 3:13 KJV

Who is wise and understanding among you? Let them show it by their good life, by deeds done in the humility that comes from wisdom.
James 3:13 NIV

The fear of the Lord is the beginning of wisdom: a good understanding have all they that do his commandments: his praise endureth for ever.

Psalm 111:10 KJV

The fear of the Lord is the beginning of wisdom; all who follow his precepts have good understanding. To him belongs eternal praise.

Psalm 111:10 NIV

Happy is the man that findeth wisdom, and the man that getteth understanding. For the merchandise of it is better than the merchandise of silver, and the gain thereof than fine gold. She is more precious than rubies: and all the things thou canst desire are not to be compared unto her. Length of days is in her right hand; and in her left hand riches and honour. Her ways are ways of pleasantness, and all her paths are peace. She is a tree of life to them that lay hold upon her: and happy is every one that retaineth her.
Proverbs 3:13-18 KJV

Blessed are those who find wisdom, those who gain understanding, for she is more profitable than silver and yields better returns than gold. She is more precious than rubies; nothing you desire can compare with her. Long life is in her right hand; in her left hand are riches and honor. Her ways are pleasant ways, and all her paths are peace. She is a tree of life to those who take hold of her; those who hold her fast will be blessed.
Proverbs 3:13-18 NIV

Witnessing

And Jesus came and spake unto them, saying, All power is given unto me in heaven and in earth. Go ye therefore, and teach all nations, baptizing them in the name of the Father, and of the Son, and of the Holy Ghost: Teaching them to observe all things whatsoever I have commanded you: and, lo, I am with you always, even unto the end of the world. Amen.

Matthew 28:18-20 KJV

Then Jesus came to them and said, "All authority in heaven and on earth has been given to me. Therefore go and make disciples of all nations, baptizing them in the name of the Father and of the Son and of the Holy Spirit, and teaching them to obey everything I have commanded you. And surely I am with you always, to the very end of the age."

Matthew 28:18-20 NIV

And he said unto them, Go ye into all the world, and preach the gospel to every creature.

Mark 16:15 KJV

He said to them, "Go into all the world and preach the gospel to all creation."

Mark 16:15 NIV

How then shall they call on him in whom they have not believed? and how shall they believe in him of whom they have not heard? and how shall they hear without a preacher?

Romans 10:14 KJV

How, then, can they call on the one they have not believed in? And how can they believe in the one of whom they have not heard? And how can they hear without someone preaching to them?

Romans 10:14 NIV

But sanctify the Lord God in your hearts: and be ready always to give an answer to every man that asketh you a reason of the hope that is in you with meekness and fear: Having a good conscience; that, whereas they speak evil of you, as of evildoers, they may be ashamed that falsely accuse your good conversation in Christ.

1 Peter 3:15-16 KJV

But in your hearts revere Christ as Lord. Always be prepared to give an answer to everyone who asks you to give the reason for the hope that you have. But do this with gentleness and respect, keeping a clear conscience, so that those who speak maliciously against your good behavior in Christ may be ashamed of their slander.

1 Peter 3:15-16 NIV

Work

And whatsoever ye do, do it heartily, as to the Lord, and not unto men. Colossians 3:23 KJV

Whatever you do, work at it with all your heart, as working for the Lord, not for human masters. Colossians 3:23 NIV

Therefore, my beloved brethren, be ye stedfast, unmoveable, always abounding in the work of the Lord, forasmuch as ye know that your labour is not in vain in the Lord. 1 Corinthians 15:58 KJV

Therefore, my dear brothers and sisters, stand firm. Let nothing move you. Always give yourselves fully to the work of the Lord, because you know that your labor in the Lord is not in vain. 1 Corinthians 15:58 NIV

Let all your things be done with charity. 1 Corinthians 16:14 KJV

Do everything in love. 1 Corinthians 16:14 NIV

Commit thy works unto the Lord, and thy thoughts shall be established.

Proverbs 16:3 KJV

Commit to the Lord whatever you do, and he will establish your plans.

Proverbs 16:3 NIV

Labour not for the meat which perisheth, but for that meat which endureth unto everlasting life, which the Son of man shall give unto you: for him hath God the Father sealed.

John 6:27 KJV

Do not work for food that spoils, but for food that endures to eternal life, which the Son of Man will give you. For on him God the Father has placed his seal of approval.

John 6:27 NIV

Whether therefore ye eat, or drink, or whatsoever ye do, do all to the glory of God.

1 Corinthians 10:31 KJV

So whether you eat or drink or whatever you do, do it all for the glory of God.

1 Corinthians 10:31 NIV

Worried

Be careful for nothing; but in every thing by prayer and supplication with thanksgiving let your requests be made known unto God. And the peace of God, which passeth all understanding, shall keep your hearts and minds through Christ Jesus.   Philippians 4:6-7 KJV

Do not be anxious about anything, but in every situation, by prayer and petition, with thanksgiving, present your requests to God. And the peace of God, which transcends all understanding, will guard your hearts and your minds in Christ Jesus.   Philippians 4:6-7 NIV

Humble yourselves therefore under the mighty hand of God, that he may exalt you in due time: Casting all your care upon him; for he careth for you.

1 Peter 5:6-7 KJV

Humble yourselves, therefore, under God's mighty hand, that he may lift you up in due time. Cast all your anxiety on him because he cares for you.

1 Peter 5:6-7 NIV

Heaviness in the heart of man maketh it stoop: but a good word maketh it glad.   Proverbs 12:25 KJV

Anxiety weighs down the heart, but a kind word cheers it up.   Proverbs 12:25 NIV

Therefore I say unto you, Take no thought for your life, what ye shall eat, or what ye shall drink; nor yet for your body, what ye shall put on. Is not the life more than meat, and the body than raiment? Behold the fowls of the air: for they sow not, neither do they reap, nor gather into barns; yet your heavenly Father feedeth them. Are ye not much better than they? Which of you by taking thought can add one cubit unto his stature?

Matthew 6:25-27 KJV

"Therefore I tell you, do not worry about your life, what you will eat or drink; or about your body, what you will wear. Is not life more than food, and the body more than clothes? Look at the birds of the air; they do not sow or reap or store away in barns, and yet your heavenly Father feeds them. Are you not much more valuable than they? Can any one of you by worrying add a single hour to your life?"

Matthew 6:25-27 NIV

But seek ye first the kingdom of God, and his righteousness; and all these things shall be added unto you. Take therefore no thought for the morrow: for the morrow shall take thought for the things of itself. Sufficient unto the day is the evil thereof.

Matthew 6:33-34 KJV

But seek first his kingdom and his righteousness, and all these things will be given to you as well. Therefore do not worry about tomorrow, for tomorrow will worry about itself. Each day has enough trouble of its own.

Matthew 6:33-34 NIV

Scripture Index

Made in the USA
Columbia, SC
22 December 2023